D1529000

GOMILLION *versus* LIGHTFOOT

BY BERNARD TAPER

The first case of its kind to be argued before the Supreme Court, Gomillion *v.* Lightfoot deals with the denial of Negro voting rights in Tuskegee, Alabama, by the gerrymandering of that township's boundaries.

Brilliantly and accurately documented, this probing report follows the case from its inception in 1957, through the personal reactions of Tuskegee's citizens as they became involved, to the Supreme Court in 1960. *Gomillion versus Lightfoot* also gives a remarkable portrait of the Supreme Court in action and of the Justices as they worked toward their final decision.

Tuskegee is a pretty, peaceful little town which is the seat of Macon County and the home of the famed Negro college, Tuskegee Institute, founded by Booker T. Washington. Here, as elsewhere throughout the deep South, politics had always been considered a white prerogative, even though Negroes were in a four-to-one majority. In recent years, though, Tuskegee's Negroes have begun making determined efforts to register as voters. To counter this threat, the Alabama State Legislature redrew the boundaries of Tuskegee, altering the shape of the city from a simple square to a curious twenty-eight-sided figure resembling a stylized sea horse. The effect was to put Tuskegee Institute outside the city limits, along with the homes of all but about four or five of the Negro voters, but leaving the white voters within the new municipal borders.

The Tuskegee Negroes immediately appealed to the courts, where the case became

(continued on back flap)

GOMILLION *versus* LIGHTFOOT

GOMILLION

versus

LIGHTFOOT

---

the Tuskegee Gerrymander Case

BERNARD TAPER

McGraw-Hill Book Company, INC.

NEW YORK   TORONTO   LONDON

GOMILLION

versus

LIGHTFOOT

the Tuskegee Gerrymander Case

BERNARD TAPER

McGraw-Hill Book Company, INC.

NEW YORK   TORONTO   LONDON

GOMILLION VERSUS LIGHTFOOT

328

T 172 g

table of contents

one
WAITING   7

two
AN EMINENTLY
REALISTIC
BODY OF MEN   71

one

WAITING

O<small>N THE AFTERNOON</small> in the fall of 1960 when I arrived for a week's stay in Tuskegee, Alabama—a pretty, once prosperous little city that has assumed a unique role in the struggle of the United States Negro for equal rights—the place, which is set tranquilly in the midst of rolling countryside about forty miles from Montgomery, looked as if there should have been a large municipal "Gone Fishing" sign hung out over Main Street. The grassy square in the center of town, with its inevitable Confederate memorial, drowsed vacantly in the bright sunshine; the stores that rimmed the square and lined Main Street were all closed. The only signs of life I saw as I walked from the Greyhound bus station to the town's one hotel, the Harris, three blocks away, were a couple of Negroes standing beside taxicabs near the bus station, and an elderly, pink-cheeked white man, with a cigar in his mouth and a pop bottle in one limp hand, lounging in a chair on the shady sidewalk in front of the hotel. After I had checked into the hotel, a rather venerable establishment on whose main floor the most striking item of decoration was a stately barber chair (which I never saw used, and which I later learned was only being kept there temporarily), and had been shown my room, with windows from which one could contemplate the red brick solidity of the Methodist Church, I got to talking with the hotelkeeper, a slim, loose-limbed man of about forty, with a flat, slow-paced style of speech. I asked him how the town happened to be so deserted on a midweek afternoon, and he replied promptly, "Bet you think it's because of the nigger boycott. Well, it ain't that. They're boycotting our stores, all right, and it's hurt us, but not all that bad. The main thing is it's Tuesday afternoon. Tuesday afternoon's when we always close up here, like most little towns in these parts do one afternoon a week. So don't you go writing that the boycott's got us paralyzed. (I had let him know that I had come to Tuskegee as a reporter for the magazine I work for—*The New Yorker.*) This town's been treated mighty unfair in the way it's been written up. Outsiders don't understand us. You really gotta live with our problem to understand it. We got nothin' against the niggers.

10

They always been treated fine here, real fine. They got their own schools, hospitals—everything—and all just as good or better than white people got. But we just want to be able to have our own town and not be swamped by the niggers. It's no joke, you'll see. I'm glad you're going to stick around a few days, because you'll find that folks here are as decent, fine people as you could ever hope to meet. What'd you do with your bags—leave them at the bus station? I'll drive you up to pick them up. No, it's no trouble—mighty glad to be able to oblige."

Genial as he was, the hotelkeeper seemed, as he spoke of these matters, to have something of an anxious, strained look about the eyes—an expression I was to notice on the faces of a good many local white people.

In Tuskegee—which is the seat of Macon County and the home of the famous Negro college, Tuskegee Institute, founded by Booker T. Washington in 1881 —Negroes have long outnumbered whites by a margin of around four to one (the city's present population is estimated to be around 6,700). The ratio for Macon County as a whole is about the same. Since Reconstruction days, the town's way of life has been the epitome of the benign paternalism that white Southerners have usually had in mind when they talked of "good race relations." It was here, during the post-Reconstruction era, that the traditional philosophy of

Negro acceptance of white political supremacy was enunciated for the South (to the relief of a North fed up with the issue of equal rights) by Booker Washington when the white supremacists were resuming power and laying the legal basis for the whole present fabric of the segregated society. Washington urged his fellow Negroes not to enter into a bitter struggle over this but to concentrate on improving and educating themselves, and to have faith that the white people of the South would gladly accord the Negro his due once he proved himself deserving of it. "Brains, property, and character for the Negro will settle the question of civil rights," he said in one speech, and, in another, "The great thing for us as a race is to conduct ourselves so as to become worthy of the privileges of an American citizen, and these privileges will come."

By now it is no news that things have not worked out so purely and simply. Even in pastoral Tuskegee, the very model and Mecca of the old way, there has arisen a fundamental challenge to the hallowed scheme of affairs, much to the surprise of white Southerners, and of many Negroes as well. In the struggle over equal rights, Tuskegee's role has been without the violent, ugly aspects of white reaction that have been seen recently in Birmingham or Montgomery, and without the dramatic confrontations evoked by the Freedom Riders or the lunch-counter sit-ins. It is a special situation, but, in its way, most revealing. The friction had been slowly developing since the Second World War, when for the first time Negroes began seeking to register to vote in appreciable numbers. (Before the war, there were less than one hundred Negroes registered as voters out of the twenty-two thousand living in Macon County.) Things began to come to a boil in 1954, when a Negro named Mrs. Jessie P. Guzman announced her candidacy for one of the seats on the Macon County School Board. Not since Reconstruction days had a Negro presumed to run for public office in Macon County, where, as elsewhere in the rural Deep South, it had been simply taken for granted that all elective offices were white prerogatives. Mrs. Guzman—who is, incidentally, director of the Department of Records and Research at Tuskegee Institute—lost to her white opponent by a margin about equal to the numerical difference between Negro voters and white voters. ("Y'see how them niggers do," a gray-haired shopkeeper remarked to me one day as he recalled this election. "They'll always vote in a bloc if you give 'em a chance.") For the white community, Mrs. Guzman's candidacy seems to have been a considerable shock, especially since it came at a time of discomforting awareness of changes brewing in the South: the school-desegregation decisions, the bus boycott in nearby Montgomery, and the news that Congress seriously intended to pass civil-rights legislation to guarantee Negro voting rights. There were at the time about six hundred registered white voters in the city and about four hundred registered Negroes. For the whites, the disquieting facts were that just about every one of the white townspeople eligible to vote had been registered, that a lot of Negroes had not been, and that many of these Negroes were not only dismayingly persistent in seeking to register but also, in many cases, dismayingly well qualified—possessed of M.A.s, Ph.D.s, and similar impressive testimonials to their literacy—and were thus a constant embarrassment to local officials conscientiously attempting to protect white supremacy. It even seemed possible that if drastic steps were not taken, the Negro electorate might eventually increase in number to the point where it would play a meaningful, even decisive, part in municipal elections. This was, it seemed, unthinkable. Accordingly, in July, 1957, it was decided to run the Negro voters out of town or, rather—since, unlike Birmingham or Montgomery, this is a peaceable spot, whose citizens believe in law and order and disapprove of physical violence—to run their residences out of town. The Alabama State Legislature drew up an ingenious new city boundary, altering the shape of Tuskegee from a simple square to a curious twenty-eight-sided figure resembling a stylized sea horse. The effect was to put Tuskegee

Institute outside the city limits, along with the homes of all but four or five of the Negro voters, while leaving all of the white voters within the municipal borders. Thus, continued white control was assured in the city proper, where it had been most threatened. Though the ejected Negroes would still be able to vote in county, state, and national elections, there were not enough of them registered as voters to influence the political situation on any scene larger than the municipal one.

The bill that accomplished this—Alabama Act 140—was passed unanimously and without debate by the legislature. If, on its face, it purported to be merely a routine redistricting measure, its central aim not only was transparently obvious but was frankly announced by its sponsor, State Senator Sam Engelhardt, Jr., of Shorter, a hamlet twenty miles from Tuskegee, who is executive secretary of the White Citizens Councils of Alabama. He had long advocated the use of the gerrymander as one surefire way for whites to keep control of the ballot box. That was a device that would withstand any court challenge, he had predicted.

To this day, the local white townspeople profess astonishment at the repercussions their gerrymander set off and at the attention it drew. (There were comments in journals as remote as the London *Economist*, which called it a piece of "mournful symbolism," in view of Booker Washington's expectations.) "I don't understand why there's been such a fuss made over us," Mrs. Hal Fisher, a plump, housewifely woman who, with her husband, edits and publishes the weekly Tuskegee *News,* told me during my stay. "Surely it's our own business what we wish our town's boundaries to be." There were ample reasons, though, for the episode to attract the widespread attention it did. To those concerned with the American Negro's efforts to improve his lot, it has become evident that the suffrage question is at the very heart of the matter. Once Negroes generally succeed in obtaining the vote, it is felt, many of their present problems will prove much easier to solve, in accordance with the fundamental social law that politicians are more considerate of people who can vote than they are of those who can't. This is the philosophy of the Civil Rights Acts that Congress passed in 1957 and 1960. But the Tuskegee episode came as a striking revelation of the lengths to which Southern states might be willing to go to vitiate the Negro's voting power when he finally does succeed in obtaining it. At the same time, the affair brought a revelation of how firmly the Negroes today intend to pursue their quest for equal rights. The Tuskegee Negroes, many of whom later told me they had been shocked not so much by the injustice of the gerrymander as by its inexcusable rudeness, responded vigorously in a wide variety of ways.

They went to law to challenge the gerrymander act's validity. Starting in the winter of 1957, when the United States Commission on Civil Rights was established, they sent in to that body a stream of petitions and meticulously documented complaints about the systematic denial of their suffrage rights—more such complaints than there were from any other county in the United States. Many of them stopped trading with Tuskegee's merchants, saying that if the town didn't want their votes, it shouldn't expect their money. This was the start of the boycott to which the hotelkeeper had referred.

I had closely followed the Tuskegee affair from the start, and one day I learned that the lawsuit it had engendered had been placed on the Supreme Court docket. The case, which was known as Gomillion et al. v. Lightfoot et al.—Gomillion being a professor at Tuskegee Institute and Lightfoot the city's mayor—was to be the first one involving a racial gerrymander that the court had ever considered, and during the time the suit had been in process, making its way slowly up through the chain of federal courts, it had become the center of a whole constellation of constitutional questions relating to suffrage rights, racial discrimination, gerrymandering in general, the powers of the states, and the limitations of the federal judiciary. Since I had become deeply interested in both the legal and social aspects of the matter, I decided to spend several days in Tuskegee looking about for myself, and then go directly on to Washington to see how the issues looked from the lofty vantage point of the Supreme Court.

Contrary to my first impression on that sleepy afternoon I arrived in Tuskegee, the townspeople had not all gone fishing. Many of the local businessmen, the hotelkeeper presently revealed, were taking part in a meeting at the City Hall. "It's something to do with a new industry the town's considering," he said. Having planned nothing for the afternoon, I thought I might as well look in on this gathering. So after a bit I walked up to the City Hall, a small, plain building tucked modestly into a niche beside the region's main repository of power, the County Courthouse—an exuberant brick edifice with a spired tower and a multitude of gables—and made my way upstairs to the meeting room. It was an unadorned chamber rather suggesting a classroom, and in it some sixty people, mostly men in shirtsleeves, were seated in eight or ten rows of chairs. I took an unoccupied seat and settled back to listen to a large, youngish man with a smooth, pudgy face and wavy silver hair, who was standing at the front of the room beside a table holding a number of variously shaped objects of burnished metal. He was talking about something called go-karts, and he was aglow with enthusiasm. "Are you folks aware, now, that the go-kart industry is the fastest-growing industry in the United States today?" he said. "Why, the Simplex Company, of Noo Orleans, has quit manufacturin' motorsickles and bisickles altogether and is turnin' out over fifteen hundred go-karts a month. They're strivin' to reach thirty-five hundred. That's a fact." The speaker, I presently discovered, was an officer of a small machine-products company that had been holding discussions with Tuskegee's Industrial Development Board about moving to Tuskegee. A go-kart (I later inspected one that was on exhibit in the hall outside) is a low-slung contraption with a steel-pipe frame, small rubber-tired wheels, and a gasoline motor—a sort of high-powered soapbox; it is used for racing on specially built tracks, which, I gathered, are being laid out all over the place. The company had developed its own go-kart model, which it hoped to market, in quantity, at a price of two hundred and forty-five dollars. "Now, there's no reason why we can't get in on the boom, because we're all ready to go," the silver-haired man went on. "It's a fad, you may say. Sure—but it's fine while it lasts, isn't it?"

I listened to all this in fascination. Go-karts, I thought, surely must be a theme about as remote as anything could be from the racial problems with which Tuskegee was beset. But after I got to know the town better I realized that the topic wasn't so utterly remote at that. Although the word "Negro" was not once spoken at the go-kart meeting, indirectly it was as a result of the racial conflict that the meeting was being held. Most Southern towns had long been actively seeking to attract industry, but Tuskegee had never made much effort in that direction until the gerrymander dispute developed. Before then the town had prospered as the market center of Macon County, and had been content with that. The Negro boycott had come as both an economic and a social shock. At the outset, local business receipts had been cut by as much as seventy per cent; some twenty firms had had to close their doors, and, although subsequently business did pick up somewhat as Negroes who disliked the inconvenience of shopping many miles away began drifting back to Tuskegee stores, it remained, at the time of my visit, about thirty per cent below normal. The Negroes' slogan for the boycott was "Buy Wisely—Trade with Your Friends!"; and they had said that any one of the town's merchants could qualify as a friend simply by expressing open disapproval of the gerrymander. None did so. Instead, the businessmen tried to cope with their predicament by more complicated means. On their behalf, Alabama's Attorney General, John Patterson—who since then has become the state's Governor and acquired world fame on a par with that of Orval Faubus—sought a court

injunction against the boycott, but the courts refused
to sustain this, declaring there was no way people
could be compelled by law to shop where they didn't
want to shop. When this move failed, the merchants
began seeking to attract new industry, motivated not
only by the need for new sources of revenue but also
by the wistful hope (expressed to me by several of
them) that the new industries would bring a large
enough number of white employees to counteract, in
time, the preponderance of Negroes in the population.
So far, Tuskegee hadn't been doing strikingly well in
this effort. In three years, only one new enterprise, a
small garment factory, had been attracted to town.
At the meeting I was attending, the officers of the
machine-products firm dwelt vividly on the poten-
tialities for future expansion, not merely in the go-
kart line but also in the manufacture of precision
machine parts and of a special clutch, for which they
predicted a great demand. But as I sat listening to
their words and to various questions from the audience,
I couldn't help feeling that there was something odd
and unpromising in the meeting's atmosphere. I was
unable to define what it was, though, until one of the
speakers, in answer to a question about the company's
finances, confessed, with an artless smile, "Frankly,
we're undercapitalized," and went on to propose that
those present sign up then and there to buy stock in the
venture. He produced a sheet of paper for the pur-

pose, and looked out expectantly over the audience, but nobody responded. It was a moment rather like the one at a carnival when the barker tries to lure the people who have just seen the free teaser up to the ticket booth and into the tent, and the crowd sheepishly melts away. There was some hemming and hawing from the Tuskegee businessmen, and then one of them, a muscular, red-headed man seated a couple of rows behind me, commented bluntly, "This meeting's drug on too long," and suggested that they adjourn, think things over, and meet for a decision the following week. I left the City Hall feeling none too impressed with such efforts as an effective solution to Tuskegee's fundamental predicament.

Returning to the hotel, I telephoned Professor Charles G. Gomillion, the chairman of the Tuskegee Institute's Division of Social Sciences and, as the leader among local Negroes concerned with obtaining equal rights, the man whose name headed the list of plaintiffs in the lawsuit pending before the Supreme Court. When I reached Gomillion, he revealed that a meeting of the town's main Negro group, the Tuskegee Civic Association, of which he was president, was to be held that evening in the Mount Olive Missionary Baptist Church, and he asked if I'd like to attend it with him. As I accepted, it struck me that this uncalculated symmetry of scheduling provided a particularly fitting way to round out my first day in town.

Since I had a couple of hours free before I was to meet Gomillion near the Tuskegee campus, I decided to take a cab and ride around a bit, in order to get some idea of how the gerrymandered city limits ran. The taxi I got belonged, I noticed, to the Good Service Cab Company, and the driver was a heavy-set Negro of about fifty who told me his name was James Cropper. The Good Service Company's cabs are what are called in the South, "colored cabs"—a term that usually has nothing to do with the color of the cab but, rather, with the color of the driver and the passengers. In most of the Deep South, it is a breach of the delicate fabric of custom—and even, in some places, of law—for a white person to ride in a colored cab. In Tuskegee, however, it happens that all the cabs are colored, since there isn't enough business to support a white cab company. Consequently, what is improper or illegal a few miles away becomes acceptable here, and white people, when they come into town on the Greyhound bus and have to take a taxi somewhere, seem to find it possible to put up with this presumed indignity in preference to walking. They may be Southerners, but they are, after all, first and foremost Americans, and Americans don't walk anywhere if they can help it.

James Cropper thought the gerrymander a strange and melancholy business, and he had no hesitation about saying so as we pursued our eccentric route. "Now heah," he would say as we made a turn, "we're in the city. This is a white district." Then, a little farther along: "At this point, the line cuts over that way and we're out of the city—there are a few colored houses along here. Now we turn left and we're back in again for a block and a half." At a glance, one district of which the city had disencumbered itself appeared to be just the kind of neighborhood most communities would consider a prime asset: large, comparatively new homes, worth, at a guess, from fifteen to thirty thousand dollars apiece, with broad lawns and neatly clipped hedges. There, Cropper told me, lived members of the Institute's faculty, and Negro doctors and other staff members of a Veterans Administration hospital nearby—many of whom had managed to obtain the vote or had shown a strong determination to do so. Farther along, we turned into a street that led to a small rise of ground, and at the top Cropper stopped the car. The street was unpaved, with some unpretentious houses spaced along it. In one of the front yards, a few Negro children were playing in the shade of some trees. A woman who was sweeping the porch of a nearby house waved to Cropper, and he waved back. "I was bohn in the city of Tuskegee, right here on this street, and I learned to tell time by the Courthouse clock," Cropper told me, nodding toward our right, where a spire was to be seen beyond a bank of foliage. "I still live heah, in a house just a few feet from where I was bohn, and I still tell time by the same clock—but I'm not in Tuskegee any more, they say. Whenever I look over there now to get the time of day, I also get reminded how much foolishness there is in the world."

He started up the cab again, and drove me along the tree-lined Old Montgomery Road to Tuskegee Institute, about three-quarters of a mile from the center of town, where I asked him to stop and let me off. I spent a pleasant interlude strolling about the campus—a spacious, tranquil place with wide greenswards and ivy-covered buildings—enjoying the soft, pleasant Alabama air.

I had arranged to meet Professor Gomillion across the street from the campus, at the office of the Tuskegee Civic Association. A stocky, brown-skinned man of about sixty, with a reserved, austere manner, he said little as he drove me to the church where the meeting of the T.C.A. (as the organization is generally called) was to be held. In this structure, a rather new building with whitewashed interior walls and beamed ceilings, were gathered about a hundred men and women, dressed in what I judged was their churchgoing best. Some appeared to be professional or professorial types; others, more weathered and simpler in garb and posture, had an unmistakable country look.

The meeting was opened in a low key by a slim, light-skinned young academic named Frank J. Toland, a member of the Institute's history department, who brought the group up to date on various topics of interest, including the news that the Supreme Court had placed Gomillion v. Lightfoot on its docket for the following week, and developments that had taken place recently in a suit that the United States Attorney General's office was bringing against the Macon County Board of Registrars, whom it accused of discriminating against Negro applicants. Toland's summary was cool and factual, and unadorned by editorial comment.

This report was followed by a hymn, sung adequately but not inspiringly by a red-robed choir, and then by the principal speaker—the Reverend T. R. Newman, a preacher from a neighboring parish. A small man with the nervous, challenging bearing of a rooster, the Reverend Mr. Newman announced his theme as "Thank God for Another Day!"—meaning, it developed, for the changes that had been taking place for the Negro of late, when viewed in perspective. He gave praise to the Lord for the fact that the back-breaking row crops, such as cotton and corn, were being replaced in the rural South by dairy farming and timber cultivation, for the achievements of African nations in gaining freedom and admission to the United Nations, and for practically everything in between. "In this changing world, the Negro must be willing—be *willing*—to go first class," he intoned, whereupon someone in the audience spoke up encouragingly, as if at a prayer meeting, "We hear you, Reverend!" Rambling in lively fashion all over the lot, the Reverend Mr. Newman worked into his speech a blast against the credit system and also a rousing plug for the Republican Party as the Negro's best hope in the South; in the course of the latter he delivered a fervent eulogy of "one of the greatest figures this country has ever been privileged to have as President, in whose debt we all stand to this day—a towering figure of surpassing wisdom and compassion." I assumed that he was talking about Abraham Lincoln, but it turned out that he meant Herbert Hoover. I must admit he surprised me there; I hadn't heard such an encomium of Hoover since I had covered a National Association of Manufacturers banquet a good many years before.

The meeting ended with another hymn, a collection, and a few routine announcements. It had lasted about an hour, and, between the studied, rather arid rationality of Professor Toland and the pep-talk looseness of the Reverend Mr. Newman, it left me with a confused impression. I had read newspaper accounts of T.C.A. public meetings, held not long after the gerrymander went into effect, which had drawn several thousand Negroes, and which the reporters had, I gathered, found stirring and purposeful. But by now, after more than a hundred of these gatherings (formally known as Crusade for Freedom meetings), the freshness and significance seemed to have gone out of this particular form of protest. The meeting I had just attended, at any rate, had struck me as desultory and routinized, as if the participants were marking time until something new should happen, and meanwhile were telling each other over again things that they already knew. It had been, I thought as I left the church, about as unpromising a meeting, in its way, as the white businessmen's get-together a few hours earlier. The radical thought crossed my mind that just possibly both sides might profit by holding their meetings in common.

PROFESSOR GOMILLION had invited me to his house for a chat after the meeting, and we were joined there by Professor Toland and by a grave-looking, soberly dressed man in his early thirties, who was introduced to me as Professor Stanley H. Smith, a sociologist. Sitting in Gomillion's small, neat living room, we at first touched politely and stiffly on conventional, vaguely intellectual topics, the familiar conversational gambits of any professorial group at a small college-town cocktail party—although in this instance without the stimulus of cocktails—Macon being a dry county. In this particular situation, however, almost any topic was bound to lead into the one ineluctable, central subject, racial discrimination. As it happened, we came to it by way of abstract art and the new art

29

museum in nearby Montgomery, which I had noticed as I passed through that city on my way to Tuskegee. No, the professors said, they couldn't tell me what kind of collection the museum had, because, being Negroes, of course they were not allowed in.

With a harsh, not very humorous laugh, Professor Smith remarked, "They don't even let us into their zoos down here in Alabama, so they're certainly not going to let us into their museums." *

Professor Toland picked up the topic, saying thoughtfully, "It's really quite remarkable to what lengths the authorities seem prepared to go in order to avoid behaving rationally. In Montgomery, you know, they have closed down the public park altogether rather than comply with a court order that Negroes must be permitted the same use of these facilities as whites. In Danville, Virginia, they did comply with a court order to let Negroes into the public library, but felt impelled to protect their cherished way of life by removing all the seats. It's most curious, really."

He spoke in the same remote, neutral tone he had used at the meeting, as if he were a scholar from Mars noting phenomena that couldn't conceivably affect him. All three of the men present, I learned, had, for their Ph.D. dissertations, done research on some

---

* As I later discovered, when I checked with the museum, Professor Smith's assumption that Negroes would not be permitted to enter was not entirely correct. Wednesdays have been set aside for Negro art lovers at the Montgomery museum.

aspect or other of the omnipresent racial theme. Gomillion's dissertation had been "Civic Democracy in the South," Smith's "The Social Psychology of Discrimination," and Toland's (on which he was still at work) "The Negro in Alabama Politics, 1867–1901." Gomillion's study made use of a "composite socio-cultural index" he had devised, involving fifteen factors by which civic democracy could be rated. With the help of this index, he had found that as far as civic democracy was concerned, Alabama ranked on the next-to-lowest rung of the ladder, just above Mississippi; he had thus proved with considerable effort, as sociologists are wont to do, what was already well known to almost everyone else. As he talked of his thesis, I thought with some wonder, as I frequently found myself doing during my stay in Tuskegee, what an odd situation this was—these Negroes using discrimination as grist for scholarship, measuring their afflictions in terms of composite socio-cultural indexes, and, like anthropologists among a tribe of primitives, recording meticulously, for publication in scholarly journals, the folkways of the whites.

Soon the conversation moved on to the local gerrymander and its implications, and to all the strategies and counter-strategies involved thereabouts in the effort to obtain the right to vote. The scholars spoke with regret of the turn that things had taken. Dr. Gomillion pointed out that, because of Booker T. Washington's

philosophy of racial accommodation, local Negroes
had never had any interest in fighting the whites. He
said, "We were proud of this community, just as the
whites were. We think it should have been possible to
move peacefully and intelligently toward a new rela-
tionship—one of true mutual respect and dignity, not
just the outer forms of these. There was a glorious
opportunity here. With such a large pool of educated
Negroes, Tuskegee could have become a model of
partnership and coöperation—if the whites had only
been flexible enough, *realistic* enough, to perceive the
possibilities. Before too many years, Negroes are
bound to obtain their citizenship rights. Wouldn't it
be more satisfactory if they got them without becoming embittered and disillusioned in the process?" He
spoke softly but crisply. There was nothing ingratiat-
ing about his manner. With his bleak eyes and thin,
ascetic mouth, he conveyed an impression of formidable determination. I began to realize why he had
been the leading figure for the past sixteen years in
the local Negro movement for equal rights.

"The whites will tell you of their conviction that
we intended to swamp them and take over just as
soon as we got enough votes to be able to do so," Dr.
Gomillion went on. "It was never our intention to run
a full slate of candidates. We didn't wish to control,
merely to share—to be able to participate freely in
our government, on the basis of merit and interest. In

a county where Negroes are in the majority, a county that has grown prosperous with the aid of taxes paid by Negroes and money spent by Negroes, is it too much to ask that we have at least *some* representation in our government—somebody on the Board of Education, on the County Board of Welfare, on the City Council? Surely there must be an intelligent middle ground between the concept of no representation at all and that of total taking over. Ideally, of course," he added, "we would like to work toward a situation in which race didn't enter into the question at all and one merely had the opportunity to vote for the best candidate, without regard to his color."

It wasn't until around the Second World War, he said, that local Negroes began to think that by not voting they had been remiss in their duties as American citizens. In the past, they had been content to accept the unusual accommodation that had been worked out—the Negro intellectuals and professionals confining their sphere of interest to Tuskegee Institute and the veterans' hospital, and completely relinquishing political and business affairs to the whites. Between the Negro middle class of Tuskegee and the Negro farmers and sharecroppers who made up the bulk of the population of Macon County, there had been very little sense of identity.

"It was the gerrymander that brought us together," Professor Smith put in. "Before that, we professional people had the feeling that it was possible for us to go downtown and obtain special privileges. When *this* happened—the gerrymander—we discovered that the whites who ran things didn't regard us as different in any significant way from the most backward members of our race, and that historically this had always been so, and we had just never faced it. We were shocked into the realization that we were still Negroes, with all the disabilities attached thereto in the sovereign state of Alabama. The country people found our comeuppance rather amusing and, I think, subtly satisfying. They didn't rub it in, but there was some chortling. 'Well, now, join us' was their attitude at the first Crusade meeting. 'Welcome home.' "

Now that Negroes had become purposeful about trying to register, Professor Gomillion went on, local and state officials had shown themselves to be equally purposeful—and infinitely resourceful—about finding ways to thwart them. Boards of Registrars had set up tedious application procedures, had disqualified Negroes on technicalities without telling them why they failed, had met irregularly, or—for long periods—not met at all. "Some boards have resigned rather than register Negroes, and despite petitions from us, Governors have been dilatory in appointing new boards, giving as a reason that they couldn't find anybody willing to serve. During a total period of four years in the past ten, Macon County has been without a Board of Registrars, and when it *has* had one, we've often had to hunt all over the place to find where it was meeting."

Professor Smith said, "One of our T.C.A. members, Mrs. Beulah C. Johnson, was hunting around for the former board one registration day, and found them in the probate judge's office, in the big walk-in vault that's used to store all the legal documents, where they were engaged in registering some white people."

Though Negro applicants had been turned down for technicalities like listing their date of birth before instead of after their place of birth on the questionnaire, Gomillion said, white applicants had passed even though they had written "Yes" in answer to Question 19 on the application—"Will you give aid and comfort to the enemies of the United States Government or the government of the State of Alabama?" Only about a thousand out of a population of fourteen thousand presumably eligible Negroes in Macon County, he said, had succeeded in registering, and the bulk of these had done so during the administration of Governor James E. Folsom—the Governor who got himself in Dutch in the South by inviting Congressman Adam Clayton Powell to the executive mansion for a drink of Scotch.

Attempts by the United States Commission on Civil Rights and the United States Attorney General's office to bring about a fundamental change in registration policy had been resisted all the way down the line. The Alabama state legislature's prompt reaction to findings by federal officials that the records of Boards of Registrars in Macon and other counties revealed wholesale discrimination had been to pass a law giving Boards of Registrars permission to destroy their records after thirty days.

"We've just had a new board appointed here, after being for eighteen months without one," Gomillion said. "It's been in existence only about four months, so we'll have to wait and see how it does. So far, I should say, things don't look too good."

At about ten o'clock, Smith and Toland said good night and left. I stayed on to talk with Gomillion a few minutes longer. I asked him about his education, and he told me that he had got his Ph.D. just last year, from Ohio State. He had also done postgraduate work at Fiske University, where he went after spending his undergraduate years at Paine College, in Georgia. He said, "I calculate that I had a total of twenty-six months of elementary-school education." His father had been a farm laborer who had never learned to read and write; his mother had gone only through the third grade in school. In the rural, poverty-stricken region of South Carolina where he had been born and brought up, free public schooling for Negro children was provided during only three months of the year; in the remaining months the youngsters were expected to help in the fields. By the time Gomillion reached the eighth grade, he was the only child in his class, all his contemporaries having dropped out to go to work; he himself quit the eighth grade after four weeks, because he decided that the teacher didn't know any more than he did. He then worked for two and a half years, saving up to go away to a secondary school attached to Paine College. He got there at last, but stayed only until the end of his sophomore year, when he ran out of money. For the next year, he worked in a post office at Philadelphia, where, one day, an elderly Negro co-worker said to him, "Son, you ought not to look forward to remaining in the post office all your life. Go back and finish college!" The injunction struck home, and, after teaching school for a while, Gomillion did go back and got his bachelor's degree at the age of twenty-eight. "And that," he concluded, "is more or less the way you go about becoming a professor if you're born a colored boy in Johnston, South Carolina."

Gomillion had phoned for a cab for me, and we went outside to wait for it. The air was balmy; it was a lovely night. I asked whether he went along with the fervent Republicanism that the Reverend Mr. Newman had advocated at the meeting. He laughed and said, "No, I'm not a Republican. I think the Democratic Party offers the best hope for the Negroes nationally, and, to be realistic, I think one has to

work within it here in the Deep South, because it is
the party in power. But I can't blame the Negroes who
feel insulted by it and become Republicans. I can
assure you that it is a difficult moment for you, if
you're a Negro, when, after going through all that you
have to go through in order to register and obtain
your precious right of suffrage, you come to vote as
a Democrat in Alabama and you go into the voting
booth and are given a ballot—an official ballot, mind
you—that has printed at the top of the Democratic
line, 'White Supremacy for the Right.' "

There are a hundred and thirty-seven counties in
the South where, as in Macon County, Negroes constitute a majority of the population (although there
is now no state where Negroes outnumber whites).
Most of these counties are in the Deep Southern states
of South Carolina, Georgia, Alabama, Mississippi,
and Louisiana, and they constitute the so-called Black
Belt—a designation that had its origin in the color
of the soil characterizing this old plantation region,
but that is now more apt to call to mind the color of
the population. Typically, these counties are rural
still, consisting of large landholdings parcelled out
among tenant farmers. The Negroes, for the most part,
work as sharecroppers or laborers, and are absolutely
dependent on the white minority for their livelihood.

Per-capita incomes are low, and years of schooling are few. In the Black Belt, few Negroes care, or dare, to try to do anything about getting the vote. At the same time, white registration tends to run around a hundred per cent of the voting-age white population— or even a little better, as in Wilcox County, Alabama, where the rolls show 2,950 whites registered out of a total eligible white population of 2,624, and not a single Negro registered out of a total presumably eligible population of 6,085. Within recent memory, only one Negro has been brave enough to even attempt to register in Wilcox County. He was a minister, and when he showed up at the registrar's office—according to testimony given at a Civil Rights Commission hearing—he was told, "Well, now, you're all right. I could register you, but to register you means that I have to register other Negroes, and for that reason it's better not to register you." In a similar Black Belt county—Lowndes County, Alabama—as of 1959 no Negro had applied in years, and no white applicant had been rejected in years. According to a Civil Rights Commission report, Mrs. Dorothy Woodruff, one of the three Lowndes County registrars, testified in 1959 that, except for filling out the application papers, white applicants were not required to demonstrate their literacy. "After we meet, we discuss it, and if their qualifications are up to par we send them their certificate," said Mrs. Woodruff. "We have never had any that haven't been up to par." When the vice-chairman of the Commission, Robert G. Storey, asked "Is that true as to both the blacks and the whites?" Mrs. Woodruff replied "We have no blacks"—meaning no black applicants. The report adds dryly, "Neither she nor Clyde A. Day, another Lowndes County registrar, could offer any explanation of why no Negro had applied for registration during their terms of office." The Commission, however, had an explanation: "Fear of physical harm, combined with economic pressure."

These rural, impoverished, backward, fear-ridden counties are the bastions and focal points of Southern resistance to any form of desegregation and to any extension of civil rights—not merely locally but wherever these may threaten, whether in New Orleans or Little Rock. Because of the South's unbalanced political structure, in which the big-city whites are apt to find themselves almost as poorly represented in the state governments as the rural Negroes, these counties speak with very loud voices indeed in the legislatures. This continues to be true even though their numbers are steadily diminishing as year by year Negroes continue to migrate out of the rural Black Belt northward and to the cities.

On the basis of the population figures, one might expect Macon County to be not only much like the other Black Belt counties but even more so, for eighty-

four per cent of its population is Negro—the highest
such percentage in the United States. Macon *is* like
the others, and it isn't. If one drives about the back-
country roads, which I did several times during my
stay, he may observe, not too many miles away from
the idealized version of colored academe that is Tuskegee Institute, ample evidence of the squalor and
apathy characteristic of the Black Belt counties. The
presence of a sizable colored bourgeoisie, such as is
to be found in the Tuskegee area, is, however, most
uncharacteristic. One observer has written, "Perhaps
more than in any other comparable area, here are the
extremes of Negro life in the South and nation today.
In this county, black hands daily perform the most
intricate and delicate surgical operations known to
medicine in the large veterans' hospital while other
black hands till the earth under conditions char-
acterized by the most primitive superstition and back-
wardness." Tuskegee Institute and the veterans' hospital not only have created an unusual body of
educated, highly skilled Negroes but have also provided them with unusual economic security. (The
bulk of the Institute's funds comes from private en-
dowment, largely Northern in origin; the hospital's
revenue comes, of course, from the federal government.) These unique elements make the situation in
Macon County both anomalous and revealing—just
as, in a laboratory experiment, the introduction into

a standard situation of an exceptional factor may be the best way of bringing to light the true nature of some physical or chemical process.

One of the differences that I noted between Macon County and the usual Black Belt county—one that continually impressed me during my stay—was the absence of menace from the atmosphere, and, more than that, the courtesy displayed in nearly all casual encounters between the races. In view of the comprehensive nature of the struggle being conducted in this region, the prevailing good manners seemed to me a most remarkable achievement. Both sides agreed on this. I spoke one day with the president of the City Council, W. Foy Thompson, and he dwelt on the point with pride. "This is a town with fine old traditions, with wonderful relations between white and colored people," he said. "Even now, good manners continue. There's been no violence, no harshness. During the time you've been here, have you heard a single complaint from any of the colored people of anything of that sort? Tell me frankly!" When I replied that I hadn't, he said with satisfaction, "You see! It's been a very one-sided affair, though. We're still giving the niggras the same garbage service, the same water and electricity service and police protection as we did before." He meant before the boycott. For the whites, the boycott has been as great a grievance as the gerrymander has been for the Negroes. "When the boycott began," Thompson explained, "we could have cut them off, but we wanted to be fair, and we've continued just as before with the Little League Recreation program for niggra children we provide in the summer." Thompson, a lean, capable-looking man in his forties who is in the insurance business, had picked me up at the hotel just after breakfast that morning and driven me out to Tuskegee City Lake, on the eastern fringe of the city —a large body of water, which he said was wonderfully stocked with game fish. There he parked, and we sat and talked while the sun sparkled on the waves. "My family's lived a long time in this town," he said. "My mother's house was built in 1829. My father had one of the largest farms in Macon County. We had seventy-five niggra families on it." He went on to describe an example of the sort of friendship between the races that, he said, was possible in the South, and that a Northerner could have no comprehension of. The friendship was that between the Thompson family and Dr. George Washington Carver, the famous Negro scientist, who worked at Tuskegee Institute until his death in 1943, and who made a major contribution to Southern agriculture through his experiments in developing hundreds of products utilizing peanuts and sweet potatoes. "My father carried Dr. Carver all over the state on the speaking trips he used to make," Thompson told me. "As a child, I was the first person Dr. Carver ever tried his peanut-oil massage on." He related this with, I thought, unfeigned pride. It had clearly meant something to him to have been of some use to the Negro scientist. "Yes," he concluded, "we've always had wonderful relations with niggras here. And I'm glad you've been able to see that there's *still* courtesy, *still* good manners."

———————————

In a way, I gathered as my stay went on, the maintenance of these civil, and outwardly pleasant, relations between the races is something that is done with mirrors—by a sort of tacit agreement to keep up, for the purpose of conducting everyday affairs, the illusion that nothing of consequence has happened. The basic issues that have arisen are simply not discussed between whites and Negroes, the reason being that this is the way the whites want to have it. When, some time after the gerrymander, a Tuskegee faculty member who had long been on cordial terms with Mayor Phil M. Lightfoot called the latter to ask for an appointment, the Mayor readily granted it, with the proviso that he would "talk about anything but politics or the city limits." An amiable conversation ensued, in which both men triumphantly succeeded in avoiding every topic of concern to either. This kind of thing is bound to make for a certain amount of strain and anxiety beneath the gracious surface, and every now and then during my stay I caught a glimpse of the inner turmoil. There was, for instance, a scene reported by the Negro housekeeper for another prominent white Tuskegee political figure. "He has never said nothin' about what's happenin'," she said. "He hasn't even asked me if I go to the Crusade meetin's. All he ever said was, one day when he came in the kitchen, 'Callie, they say we don't like the colored people. Don't you believe that. I was raised up with colored people and I love the colored people.'"

Not only did the whites decline to discuss the race problem with Negroes, they didn't even discuss it among themselves if they could avoid it. Apparently, they hoped that if it were ignored, it would go away and life in Tuskegee would become once again as they remembered it—harmonious, prosperous, civilized, with everyone, white or black, contentedly filling his allotted place. To at least a few white persons I came to know in Tuskegee, this seemed an incredibly unrealistic course. One of them was a Presbyterian minister named James K. Thompson—a young man with an athletic build, curly yellow hair, and eyes of an extraordinarily vivid blue, who had got the call to the ministry while serving as a fighter pilot during the Korean War. As the Reverend Mr. Thompson and I sat talking one day in the study of his church, he said, "Recently, a number of civic and welfare groups got together to form an organization called the Macon

County Improvement Association. We had a meeting to discuss the areas of our concern. We talked about programs to combat juvenile delinquency and about plans for getting a new nursing home. Well, juvenile delinquency is not a problem of any dimension down here—it just isn't, fortunately. But race is. That's the greatest problem any of us have to face. Yet the Macon County Improvement Association has never discussed it. None of us are facing it."

He himself, at the time I talked with him, seemed to be wrestling with his conscience—wondering aloud whether as a Christian he ought to be speaking out publicly far more forthrightly than he had till then. "Once a year—in February—our church has a Race Relations Day," he said. "You can feel tension mounting among the congregation for weeks beforehand. Then the day comes, and I deliver a bunch of platitudes and gradually things simmer down." Nevertheless, he was hopeful. "The change is coming, whether we like it or not, from a paternalistic society to one in which there is responsible participation, and if only we can regard the prospect as a challenge, not as a threat, we can do all right here," he went on. "The South has many wonderful qualities. We have values that you in the North have lost. There's more warmth here; personal relationships mean more. The North's way of life—so impersonal and mechanical, so full of stresses and material goals—is far from ideal. It seems to me that if we here in the South can just work out this race-relations problem, we may have something to offer the country—a better, richer way of life than it has yet seen."

I didn't find many other white people, though, who were capable of treating the race-relations problem as a challenge rather than as a threat. Certainly Mayor Lightfoot was not in the least stimulated by the eminence that the case of Gomillion v. Lightfoot had conferred on him. His term of office was ending, and he was tired. "Somebody else is going to have to work this thing out," he said, with a weary sigh, one afternoon when I called on him at his home—the Varner-Alexander mansion, which is the prize antebellum house of the region. "Not me. I'm too old." He was actually about sixty, a gentlemanly figure, with sparse gray hair and a trim gray mustache. He wore a rather wistful expression. A few weeks before my arrival in town, he had been defeated for reelection, after serving for seven years as mayor, by a political newcomer—a lumberyard foreman by trade. Lightfoot was still brooding over the election result, which he said had saddened him, not for personal reasons, but because of what it signified. The working people, it appeared, were no longer content to be governed by the gentry. "They want to get their own kind in there now," he said. As I sat and listened to his wistful musings in this elegant mansion, with its colonnaded verandas;

47

its lofty rooms whose ornately carved French windows opened onto gardens in which flourished hundred-year-old camellias; its Empire furniture; its glistening chandeliers: its silverware, bought from Tiffany in 1856, laid out carefully on the sideboard, I could not help thinking how Faulknerian the scene was. I might have been listening to a Sartoris lamenting the rise of the Snopeses.

It was, of course, during Lightfoot's regime that the gerrymander had been effected, but the Mayor had little to say to me about it, or about the Negroes' new determination to be represented in their government. Probably he was still digesting his surprise at the ordinary white people's wish to be represented. What an unlikely fate had befallen this gentleman—I thought as I sat there with him—that he should pass into history forever linked, in the indexes of the lawbooks, with the Negro Gomillion.

As Gomillion had predicted, I found that nearly all the white people with whom I discussed the gerrymander justified it on the ground that *something* had had to be done to keep the Negroes from taking over completely and "swamping" them. Just exactly what effect it would have on their daily lives to be swamped nobody explained clearly, nor did anyone clarify why it should be considered appalling for a minority to be swamped by a majority but perfectly all right for a majority to be swamped by a minority, as the Negroes had been for so long. Yet there was no denying that the whites' anxiety, however shapeless, was real. None of the whites could conceive of the possibility that the Negroes, if they should ever attain power, would deal fairly with them. The most anguished revelation of this came from a businessman with whom I had several conversations. All week he had been telling me how well the Negroes had always been treated in Tuskegee, and what wonderful facilities had been provided for them, and how little trouble they would give if it were not for agitators. Then we got around to speculating on what things might be like if Negroes did succeed in registering to vote in large numbers. "That mustn't happen! It mustn't!" he said. I asked if he didn't think it possible that his fears were exaggerated—that if Negroes got into office they might treat white citizens with justice. "Well, they wouldn't," he said. "They couldn't!" But how could he be so sure, I asked. He burst out, "Listen, if there's such a thing as hate, there's gotta be hate in the nigger's heart for the white man in the South!"

In Ralph Ellison's brilliant and disturbing novel about the American Negro, *Invisible Man,* there are several scenes that take place in what is obviously the Tuskegee region—where, in fact, the author went to college. In one, a wretched country Negro named Jim

Trueblood, an inhabitant of a miserable shack on a scrubby piece of land (I had seen innumerable shacks just like it on trips through the back country not far from the Institute), gets both his wife and his daughter with child. When the Negroes up at the college hear of this, they are horrified and want to chase Trueblood out of the county. He expects the whites to deal even more harshly with him, but instead they give him food and clothing and more work than he's ever had before, and they get a big kick out of hearing him tell how he had defiled his daughter while half asleep. They practically make a pet of him. "That's what I don't understand," he says wonderingly. "I done the worse thing a man could ever do in his family and instead of chasin' me out of the county, they gimme more help than they ever give any other colored man, no matter how good a nigguh he was. Except that my wife an' daughter won't speak to me, I'm better off than I ever been before ... The nigguhs up at the school don't like me, but the white folks treats me fine."

The grim point Ellison is making is that a depraved Negro is a great comfort to the whites in the Deep South, for his existence tends to justify the superior status and privileges they enjoy—whereas educated, respectable Negroes like the ones in Tuskegee are a burden on the white man's conscience, for he finds it much harder to explain to himself why they are not to be trusted with the same rights as white people. The gerrymander was taken by the Negroes of the Tuskegee region as an implicit statement of this attitude. If they needed convincing on the point, it was made even more manifest during hearings of a legislative committee headed by State Senator Engelhardt, the man who introduced the gerrymander bill. The function of this group was to consider the possibility of abolishing Macon County altogether if the uppity Negroes there continued pestering for the vote. The committee's deliberations resulted in a bill permitting the abolition of the county at such time as the legislature might choose, and this measure, approved by Alabama voters in a state-wide referendum on December 17, 1957, has since been held in abeyance as a reserve weapon against the Tuskegee Negroes. The political reporter for the Montgomery *Advertiser* attended hearings on the bill that were held in each of the counties bordering Macon to discuss what kind of problems its abolition would entail and how it might best be divided up among its neighbors, and he told me that these hearings were about as extraordinary a spectacle as he had ever witnessed, what with the horse trading among county officials over which parts of Macon they wanted to annex and which ones they didn't. "Everybody wanted Notasulga [a region where the Negroes are most backward]," the reporter told me. "Nobody wanted Tuskegee Institute."

ON MY LAST DAY in Tuskegee, before leaving for Washington to hear the gerrymander case argued before the Supreme Court, I had a chance to see for myself what a voter-registration day in Macon County was like. It was the third Monday of the month, and thus the regularly scheduled meeting day for the County Board of Registrars. The date being October 17, this would be the last opportunity to register for those wishing to cast a ballot in the Presidential election. By now, having heard as much as I had about the difficulties that faced Negroes trying to become voters, and knowing that the United States Attorney General's office had accused the local board of discriminatory practices, I was naturally curious to observe the board's procedures. So right after breakfast that morning I set off for the Courthouse, where the board would meet. The clock in that building's spire—the clock James Cropper told time by—was striking nine as I approached. The grass looked very green in the bright sunshine, the air was fresh, and there were birds singing and rustling in the elms and magnolias. It was going to be another nice day. I went into the Courthouse and, following the directions I had been given, up a narrow, twisting stairway near the back of the building to a landing on the second floor, where fifteen or twenty people, nearly all Negroes, were waiting. The landing was lit by a naked bulb hanging at eye level from a long cord; the walls, divided by a waist-high molding, were painted a pale shade of green below and beige above; the floor was of rough, unpolished wood. There were three or four wooden chairs on the landing, and these were occupied; the rest of the applicants were standing about in small groups. On one wall was a large white card on which was roughly hand-printed, in red, "NO LOITERING."

The first person I recognized as I glanced about was Stanley Smith, the young Tuskegee sociologist whom I had met at Gomillion's. He was wearing a conservative dark-blue suit, whose hue very nearly matched the color of his skin. A Phi Beta Kappa key gleamed from his watch chain. I greeted him and asked jokingly if he was wearing his key to impress the registration board. With a thin, academic smile, he replied that he doubted the board's susceptibility to that kind of impression. Standing nearby I noticed the young white Presbyterian minister, the Reverend Mr. Thompson, and his wife, a pretty blond girl in a skirt and white shirt.

After a moment, a door across the landing opened. A stocky white man in shirtsleeves appeared and asked abruptly, in the manner of a bus conductor, "Any transfers?"—a question designed to ascertain whether anyone present had already been registered as a voter in another Alabama county and was now seeking to transfer his registration to Macon County. The Reverend Mr. Thompson nodded, and the stocky white man beckoned him and Mrs. Thompson inside.

"That's Wheeler Dyson, chairman of the new Board of Registrars," Smith told me. He went on to say that the board had started work right at nine, and that the first Negro applicant, a man named James Smith, had been admitted to the registrars' office a few minutes before my arrival. "He was No. 15 on the waiting list," the sociologist said. "My own number is seventeen. This board has instituted a new system. When you first show up, they have you sign your name on a waiting list and give you a number. Then, on subsequent registration days, they go down the list, calling the applicants in numerical order. The registrars use a tiny office, in which, they say, they can handle only one or two applicants at a time, and the applicants who do succeed

in getting in there go through interminable procedures.
I received my number on June 20th. The board has met
here three times in the four months since then, and they
still haven't got to seventeen. I've been here waiting
every time."

I asked if he thought he stood a chance of getting in
that day.

"We shall see," he said, in the tone of an interested
but detached observer, a sociologist studying a social
process in which he himself happened to be involved.

A sheet of paper was posted on the glass pane of
the door to the registrars' office, and I went over to it
and saw that it was a schedule of registration days. In
all, the board had met twelve times in the four months
since it had begun to function—three of those times
in the Courthouse, and the rest in the rural precincts.
Throughout that period, as far as was generally known,
the board had certified only eight people as voters—
five whites and three Negroes. I was reminded of an
extrapolation that William P. Mitchell, the chairman
of the Tuskegee Civic Association's voter-franchise
committee, had made in a letter he had sent to Governor
Patterson recently. Mitchell, an assiduous man in his
late forties, with a personality that combines a stubborn
devotion to a cause with a bookkeeper's penchant for
order and seemliness, has for years been doing his
meticulous best to carefully record and document the
loose procedures of the various county boards of reg-

istrars he has had to contend with. These records he sends on to the Governor, on the supposition that the Governor should be as pained as he at the erratic methods revealed. In the letter in which he made his extrapolation, he drew the Governor's attention to the fact that at the board's present rate of operation only thirty Negroes per year would be able to make application, and that the county had lost sixty-four registered Negro voters the previous year by death or departure, so, assuming that an average of thirty applicants per year were approved and registered (an extremely optimistic assumption), "if our losses continue at sixty-four per year, there will be no Negro voters in this county by 2017 A.D." Governor Patterson did not acknowledge the letter.

Looking around the anteroom, I saw that there was another white person on hand, and that he also was someone I had come to know during my week in Tuskegee. He was the man I had seen on the day of my arrival, sitting in a chair on the sidewalk in front of the hotel. I had since discovered that his name was Henry G. Jones, that he was retired, and that he spent much of his time in that chair, a cigar in his mouth, his legs stretched out before him, contemplating with idle interest whatever there was to be seen. He was now seated in his usual way, in a chair off to one side of the hallway, and was wearing his usual clothes—cream-colored pants, a brown jacket, and a blue tie on which glistened a pattern of shiny blue dots. I went over to say hello and to inquire what had brought him there. He said he wanted to transfer his vote from his native Coosa County to Macon County, and he asked if I knew how long the process took. I said that I didn't, but that he would very likely have his turn after the Thompsons came out. "I didn't have to wait at all the first time I registered," Jones remarked. "Whole thing didn't take but five minutes." He sucked reflectively on his unlit cigar. "Forty-five years ago, that was."

A group of four Negro men were standing by the staircase, and I went over to talk to them. One was a young bachelor of science from Alabama State College, who said he had lately been looking for a teaching job; the three others had the appearance of workingmen. The dominant figure in the group seemed to be an erect, slim, muscular man of about fifty who was wearing a light-blue polo shirt. He had a bony face with skin like black emery paper, taut and roughened-looking. His name, he told me, was Benjamin Hicks, and he worked at the veterans' hospital as a fireman. He said he'd been trying to get registered in Macon County for about five years. The number he'd been given by the present board was 85, so it seemed it was going to be quite a long while yet before he could expect to get in to make his application. I asked if he could tell me why he was willing to put up with all the trouble and inconvenience it took to get registered.

He answered, "Because I want to be a *citizen*, that's why, a bona-fide citizen, an active part of the government of these our United States. That government, we are told, is ours—'we, the people'—but as long as I cain't vote, I'm outside it, not doing my share. Now, I don't like not doing my share."

One of the other men put in, "That's right!"—like an amen.

"I was bohn here," Hicks went on, "and my fore-parents were bohn here. I own a home here and farming land, too, and pay taxes on 'em, and I just paid taxes on my car." He waved a cellophane-wrapped car license he was holding in his hand. "But yet I have no say in what's done with my taxes. That ain't right. I lived a while in Illinois once. Up there they *beg* you to register. It don't make sense to me that a strange state will let me vote but my own home state won't." He made these points not in an aggrieved voice but, rather, with the even emphasis of one who simply states the indubitable. "Mind you, now, I'm just an ordinary person, and this ain't an issue with me, or a big *crus*ade. It's just that as an ordinary person I want to be part of everything I'm entitled to be part of."

The others nodded agreement, and again one of the bystanders chimed in with "That's right!"

The young graduate, leaning on the banister a step above us, said, "I'm going to stay here all day today, just the way I stayed all day last time, and I'll stay all day next time and as long as it takes till I get in that office there."

About forty minutes had passed since I had arrived on the scene, and during that time several more Negroes had shown up. The ones who were making their first appearance since the new board had begun to function were directed by the others to knock on the office door, and then sign their names on the waiting list. When they came out after doing so, they were asked what numbers they had got, and there was a good deal of speculation on how soon they could expect to be called. The latest applicant to emerge from the office was a slight man of about thirty, wearing a dark suit. An expression of irresistible mirth glowed on his shiny, round, bespectacled face. When he was asked what number he had got, he giggled and displayed a card on which was stamped the number 94. "I'm going to save this for my son—my unborn son," he said, spluttering with laughter. "The board should just about be up to No. 94 when he turns twenty-one and begins to think about getting registered."

A tall, tan-colored man wearing tinted glasses remarked, "I've got No. 68. Does that mean I should come back in 1968?"

A woman put in soberly, "How do we know these numbers will be good even next year? This is the first time a board has used numbers. What's to stop them from saying at the start of next year that these numbers were just for this year and we've got to begin all over again?"

The mirthful young man replied, "We must have faith in the board's good intentions."

I started to stroll about the landing, and as I passed near Henry G. Jones, the retired white man, he asked me, "Say, how long does this business take, anyway? I think I'll run along. I'm not going to waste the whole day sitting around here."

At this, a couple of the Negroes nearby spoke up, urging him not to rush off. "It can't be more than a few minutes longer now for you, since you're just transferring. You surely want to get your *vote,* don't you?" one of them said, in a tone that made the vote sound like a most precious possession indeed. The situation was, of course, loaded with irony—these Negroes, for whom getting the vote was practically a lifetime occupation, seeking to persuade this elderly white man with time on his hands not to give up so easily— but those present said nothing about the irony, if they perceived it. Grumbling a little, Jones let himself be persuaded. Sure enough, a few minutes later the Thompsons came out of the office and departed, and the registrar signalled to Jones to come in.

There was still no sign of James Smith, the Negro who had gone into the office at nine to make his application. Some of the Negroes told me that, to judge by the experiences of others they knew who had attempted to register, he would not yet have started filling out his application form, but would still be copying page after page of the Constitution of the United States in longhand to prove his literacy. This is a requirement that many Negroes find particularly rankling, and as I walked around, after Jones had gone in, I heard some of the people on the landing talking about it.

A large, hearty-looking woman in a green dress said to a middle-aged, neatly attired man who looked like a professor, "They should use some other book, not the Constitution. It's an insult to the Constitution to use it they way they do."

"I can understand why one must demonstrate his literacy," the professorial-looking man replied. "But certainly it shouldn't have to take me an hour and a half or two hours of reading and writing to prove that I can cope with the English language. It didn't take me that me that long to demonstrate my competence in French—and German as well, for that matter—when I took my Ph.D. exams at Boston University." He was a squarely built, tan-colored man with broad features and a high, domed forehead, who, from his style of speech, manifestly had a vested interest in rhetoric. I learned that he was Daniel W. Wynn, the Tuskegee Institute's chaplain and also a professor of philosophy there. He said that he held No. 58, and that today was his fifth attempt to register in Tuskegee. (Previously, he said, he had registered without difficulty in Massachusetts and Texas. Quite a number of those present, I gathered, had voted in other states.) Once, during the previous board's tenure, he had succeeded in getting in to apply, but had heard nothing further. After waiting a few months, he had gone back to ask what had happened to his application. "The registrar I saw didn't bother to look up my application," Wynn said. "He just said, in an offhand way, 'Well, if you haven't heard, you didn't pass.'"

In Wynn's vicinity on the landing, most of the academics and professionals seemed to be gathered: Stanley Smith, the sociologist; the mirthful young man, who proved to be D. T. Williams, one of the Institute's librarians, and to have an M.A. from the University of Illinois; Henry Pennymon, the tall man with tinted glasses, who had an M.A. from the University of Michigan in industrial-arts education; Mrs. Charlotte Lewis, a lawyer; Mrs. Lois Reeves, the stout, hearty woman in green, who was about to get her M.A. in social welfare; and a couple of others. On some registration days here, I knew, there had been so many people with advanced degrees waiting that an outsider coming on the scene might have thought he'd stumbled into a meeting of the Modern Language Association. Today, though, the group was less heavily academic; along with the professors and the people I had already talked to, the would-be applicants whom I met during the morning included an unskilled laborer, some artisans, a couple of clerical workers, several housewives, and three or four farmers.

Time passed slowly. Most of the people on the landing chatted among themselves as the morning wore on. A housewife sat reading a *Ladies' Home Journal*. A young woman who looked like a college student was reading a paperback. Several people sat or stood quietly—not talking or reading, just waiting. It was a curious atmosphere, neither passive nor impatient. These people seemed to have settled down to their waiting as to a kind of chosen occupation—something that they had learned well how to do. They were formidable at it.

At ten-thirty, the elderly white man, Jones, came out of the registrars' office and went his way. There was still no sign of the Negro who had gone in at nine o'clock. At ten-forty, Dyson, the registrar, opened the door, put his head out, and looked around. Then he drew it back in and closed the door. Five minutes later, he looked out again. He had done this several times during the morning, his face always wearing a frown. "You people clear the hallway, please!" he now called out. "Go on in the courtroom—it's empty. You all know nobody's supposed to loiter here." He drew his head back and closed the door.

None of the people on the landing moved, or commented on this order. It was as if they hadn't heard it. They just went right on doing whatever they had been doing.

I went over to Professor Smith and asked, "Aren't you people going to do as he says?"

Smith laughed. "No, of course not! We're going to stay right here where he can see us whenever he peeps out."

I remarked that Mr. Dyson looked a bit unhappy.

"Of course he's unhappy," Smith said. "How could he not be unhappy? He'd like nothing better in the world than to peep out sometime and find that, by some miracle, we've all vanished and are never going to trouble him again. But no, whenever he peeps out, there we still are—poor man." He laughed again, a rather brusque laugh. "It's a tragicomedy down here, you know," he said.

I mentioned something I had been feeling more and more strongly as the morning went on—that I found the kind of quiet persistence exhibited by these people very moving. It was an ordeal by boredom with which they were being tried, and that can sometimes be a greater test of one's mettle than an ordeal by danger.

"Yes, I know what you mean," Smith said. "These are obscure, unsung people. They're not looking to be heroes, but they do what has to be done." He was, of course, one of them, despite his detachment. "They aren't fooling themselves," he went on. "Nearly every one of them knows he's not going to get into the registration office today. But they all want the State of Alabama to know that they don't acquiesce in this system or approve of it, that they're not going to be kept out forever."

Many of them, I knew, had not found it easy to arrange to spend a day here. I asked Smith about himself —didn't he have classes today?

"Oh, yes, three classes. I've rescheduled them, and we'll meet this evening—at six, seven, and eight o'clock. When I have to do this, I let my students know. I explain why I'm doing it. It's part of their sociological education, you might say."

About eleven-thirty, a few people began drifting away. The stout woman in green apologized for leaving but said she had to meet her mother, who was arriving by train. "It's a conflict of values," she said. James Smith, Applicant No. 15, was immured in the office, as he had been since nine. At a quarter past twelve, Professor Smith remarked to me, "This is the first time I've known the board to work later than noon." A moment or two later, James Smith emerged from the office. The Negroes clustered around him, asking him how it had gone, and whether he had managed to complete his application, and how he was feeling. They treated him rather as if he were the survivor of some hazardous ordeal—someone who had just succeeded in making his way to safety after being lost in the woods, or had endured a fortnight on a drifting raft in perilous seas.

"That's probably the only applicant the board will have time to take this morning," Professor Smith remarked to me. "Another one ought to get in this afternoon, but there's no guaranteeing he'll finish all the writing they assign him by the end of the day. So it doesn't look as if I'm going to get in to apply today, either. Maybe next month I'll make it. There'll probably be another twenty or thirty Negroes showing up this afternoon to get on the list. Heavens knows when *they'll* get in. By the end of today, the accomplishments will be perhaps two transfers of white people and two completed applications from Negroes. On the average, in the past, the board has been certifying about one Negro out of every three who apply. On that basis, by the end of the day they will have managed to register something like two-thirds of a Negro."

A few minutes after the applicant had emerged, Dyson came out of the office, followed by another white man—a younger man who, I was told, was the other registrar, Charles Scott. The two checked to see that the office door was locked behind them, and then started down the stairs. I hurried after the pair, and when I caught up with them, I introduced myself and said I would appreciate an opportunity to interview them. The younger man turned on his heel and stalked off.

Dyson gave me a baleful look. He wasn't going to talk
to me, he said as I walked beside him through the
Courthouse hall, because he had nothing to say and
because most reporters weren't interested in printing
the truth. Nevertheless, after he had got outside and
into his car, he did not start the motor immediately, but
sat looking through the open window at me, waiting
for me to ask a question.

"Mr. Dyson," I said, "as chairman of the Board of
Registrars, do you have any constructive proposals or
suggestions for speeding up the registration proce-
dure?"

He blinked, then peered sidewise at me suspiciously.
At last, he said, "Them niggras ought to learn to write
faster." After a moment, he added, in an aggrieved
tone, "You ought to see some of the people they're
tryin' to push through."

I said I understood that some of the Negroes the
board had rejected had Ph.D. degrees.

Dyson replied, "Well, they missed some part of the
questionnaire. If a fella makes a mistake on his questionnaire, I'm not gonna discriminate in his favor just
because he's got a Ph.D." He spoke righteously, a man
who had found a cause: no discrimination in favor of
Ph.D.s. "We treat everybody alike, white or black," he
went on. "Nobody can say we're not treatin' everybody exactly equal." He gave me a challenging look.
A ruddy-faced man with glasses, he sat with his brawny

arms braced on the steering wheel. I was aware, in the drowsy noonday quiet that lay over the scene, of some birds singing amiably in a nearby tree. A couple of people strolled by. "Look here, I've worked with niggras," Dyson said. "I know 'em. I got nothin' against em'. I get along good with 'em personally." To this I made no response, since for all I knew it might be perfectly true. After a moment he burst out, "I don't see what all the fuss is about. They claim there's fourteen thousand niggras of voting age in the county. Yet in the four months our board's been operatin', only ninety-five niggras have come in to apply." This he brought forth triumphantly, to prove there was no real, widespread desire on the part of Negroes to become voters, and that suggestions to the contrary were specious propaganda. "Anyway," Dyson went on, "we're not doing so badly. We're new at this. It takes a while to get procedures set up and all that. If people would just let us alone, we'd work this thing out all right." He said this with great feeling. I didn't at all doubt his sincerity, and again, as when I saw him poking his head out of his office door, I couldn't help feeling rather sorry for him.

"Is it really necessary to have such lengthy registration procedures?" I asked.

"The laws of the State of Alabama require applicants to show that they can read and write the Constitution."

"I thought the law said 'read *or* write,' " I said.

"Well," he said, "the law says the board may, at its discretion, require applicants to do both."

"Even so, why couldn't you use a larger room for registration, in which you could take ten or twenty people at a time—a classroom, or the courtroom itself?" I asked.

"The room we got's the only one they give us," he replied.

"Who's 'they'?"

"The Courthouse," he said, mysteriously, and then he returned to his theme that conditions were just the same for white and black, so there was no reason to complain.

After a moment, I thanked him for the interview and stepped back from the car. He started the engine. "People ought to let us alone," he said, and, frowning, backed the car out of its parking place and drove off for his lunch.

two

AN EMINENTLY REALISTIC
BODY OF MEN

THE ARCHITRAVE above the porticoed entrance to the United States Supreme Court Building bears the inscription EQUAL JUSTICE UNDER LAW. While one ascends the broad expanse of marble steps, as I found myself doing on the afternoon of October 18, 1960, he has time to ponder this motto—to consider the importance given to the concept of equality, to note the subtlety with which "justice" is given precedence over "law" and yet is inextricably interwoven with it. Well before I had reached the top of the steps, I had concluded that those were good words up there, beautifully put together.

Some time this afternoon the court was due to begin deliberations on the first case involving the question of a racial gerrymander ever to come before it—the case of Gomillion v. Lightfoot. All week previously, in Tuskegee, I had looked at the matter up close—embedded in all its human complexities, irrationalities, passions, aspirations, and fears. Now I was to see how it looked from a longer perspective, with its legal questions lifted out and isolated as much as possible from its emotional ones. I had left Tuskegee the evening before to hear the case argued. In Washington, now, I found that Tuskegee still clung to me. The town had made a strong impression on me, and throughout the court sessions that followed I experienced a curious sensation—as if I were in two places at once. The Tuskegee landscape seemed present in the courtroom, and I saw constantly in my mind those named in the litigation: the Negro leader Charles G. Gomillion, with his austere mouth and bleak, determined eyes, who had been born in poverty, the son of an illiterate farm laborer, and had become chairman of the Division of Social Sciences at Tuskegee Institute; Phil M. Lightfoot, the gentlemanly white Mayor of Tuskegee, as he had looked when I had visited in his elegant ante-bellum mansion a few days before and when I had heard him musing wistfully over his recent defeat for reelection; and many of the others named in the action, who were classified under the "et al."'s in its full title—C. G. Gomillion, et al., Petitioners, v. Phil M. Lightfoot, as Mayor of the City of Tuskegee, et al. The names of these people were on the lawsuit symbolically, but, having once met them, I found myself forever barred from being able to think of them symbolically; the strong flavor of their individual humanity kept obtruding itself on me, as I think it would have on anyone—except, perhaps, a born lawyer.

I had previously obtained a card admitting me to a section of the court galleries reserved for visiting journalists, and one of the guards now led me down a narrow corridor along which several doors were set close together. The guard opened one of these for me, and I found myself in one of a number of narrow stalls—rather like the boxes in Paris theatres—ranged along one side of the courtroom. A case was in progress. It dealt with the question of whether the United States government had the right to deport an alien who, long after his naturalization, had been discovered to have made a false denial of his membership in the Communist Party during naturalization proceedings. This was the first case that week. I had already glanced over the court's schedule, and had marvelled at the number and diversity of the problems with which the justices were expected to cope. After this would come the Tuskegee case; to be followed by the case labelled United States v. Mississippi Valley Generating Company, which involved the matter of conflict of interest in the negotiation of a contract under which electric power was to be delivered to a project of the

Atomic Energy Commission, and which was better known as the Dixon-Yates case; then there was a case in which a film corporation was contesting the right of the city of Chicago to censor moving pictures; and a case in which a seaman named Thomas Michalic was contesting the refusal of lower courts to award him damages against Cleveland Tankers, Inc., after he had suffered personal injuries when a wrench fell on the "big toe of his left foot"—and so on, to the extent of perhaps a hundred and fifty such widely varying cases on which the court would hear oral argument during its nine-month term, as well as fourteen hundred or so cases that it would consider in more cursory fashion.

Although I had long been interested in the Supreme Court—this institution that Professor Charles L. Black, Jr., of the Yale Law School, has called "the chief curiosity and pride and exasperation of the American system of government"—I had never before had occasion to attend a court session. I looked about me now, taking stock: there was the spacious, high-ceilinged chamber, walled with marble, trimmed with mahogany, and hung with curtains of dark-red velours; the impressive row of black-robed justices on the raised dais; the attorney standing below them, arguing his case; the other attorneys seated in several rows behind him; and then, beyond a low rail, the seats occupied by the public. All was much as I had imagined it would be, with one exception—the spectators. The entire time I was present, there was a constant wash in and out of the courtroom of tourists, most of them in sports clothes and with cameras slung from their shoulders. Few of them stayed long enough to get much idea of the case being heard, but while they were there, they sat quietly, with solemn, respectful expressions on their faces, as if they were having an experience that they were sure would do them good. As for the justices, they paid no attention to this coming and going; it didn't seem to distract them in the least.

I found that I recognized three of the justices readily: Chief Justice Earl Warren, large and majestic-looking; Felix Frankfurter, who was at the moment doing most of the questioning, in a high, precise, rather acidulous voice; and William O. Douglas, with his plainsman's weather-beaten features. One of the nine places was completely hidden from my sight behind a stack of lawbooks on the long desk. I knew that it was occupied, though, because once or twice I heard a voice emanating from behind the books. With the aid of a sort of illustrated roster (names and numbers of all the players) the court's press officer had thoughtfully given me, I determined that the owner of the voice was Justice Hugo L. Black, and I was also able to sort out the other justices—

Thomas C. Clark, John Marshall Harlan, William Joseph Brennan, Jr., Charles Evans Whittaker, and Potter Stewart.

At about 4 P.M., there was a sudden stir in the attorneys' section, and I saw that the lawyers who had been sitting in front were giving way to some of those who had been waiting in the rows behind, in a sort of hurried, unceremonious changing of the guard. Then, in a conversational tone, the Chief Justice said, "Gomillion versus Lightfoot," and a slim young Negro attorney rose to talk about Tuskegee. I had not even been aware that the arguments in the deportation case were nearing their conclusion. I had somehow supposed that between cases—and particularly between cases as different as these two were—the justices would require at least a moment or two of reflection in which to order their thoughts about the case they had just heard and to summon to mind what they had read in preparation for the new one. But, no. The court has no time to spare; too many cases of crucial import are pending—cases that may have been seeking resolution for years as they progressed upward through the nation's judiciary system.

Gomillion v. Lightfoot itself had been three and a half years en route to Washington. In all that time, the case itself had not yet come to trial anywhere.

The bulk of the litigation had been over the question of whether it was the kind of case that could properly be brought to trial in a federal court. The District Court in Montgomery, Alabama, had dismissed the Negro plaintiffs' action, holding that even if they could prove their allegations at a trial, there was nothing whatever a federal court could do about the matter—except, perhaps, sympathize with them. But no relief could be granted for their complaint. The Fifth Circuit Court of Appeals, in New Orleans, had affirmed this ruling. These courts had declared, in effect, that the State of Alabama, or any other state, has an absolute right to rearrange the boundaries of any of its cities or other political subdivisions in any way it sees fit, and that a federal court cannot question the action, regardless of the motive behind it or the arbitrariness of the action's effect. This, the courts had said, was the law as the Supreme Court had historically enunciated it; such matters as local boundaries were what Justice Frankfurter, in a 1946 case known as Colegrove v. Green, had called "a political thicket," and, as Justice Frankfurter had then written, federal "courts ought not to enter this political thicket."

The lower courts had, of course, been cognizant that gerrymandering—the drawing or redrawing of political boundaries to serve the special interests of the group in political control—is an ancient and widespread abuse, by no means confined to Alabama or to the South. The earliest recorded instance of it in America occurred in 1709, when several Pennsylvania counties tried by this means to deprive Philadelphia of its proper representation in the colonial legislature. The practice was then without a name. The name was coined about a hundred years later, in Massachusetts, when Elbridge Gerry was Governor. Gerry's party rearranged the state's political districts in a manner exceedingly advantageous to itself, carving one district into a shape as curious as that bestowed in 1957 on Tuskegee. An indignant member of the opposition party complained that the district looked like a veritable salamander, to which another retorted, "Better say a gerrymander!" The artist Gilbert Stuart drew a cartoon called "The Gerrymander" for use in the subsequent election campaign, and the word stuck. It is because of gerrymandering and legislative malapportionment (which is, roughly, gerrymandering by inertia) that the United States, though it has become a preponderantly urban nation, remains to so large an extent under the sway of rural lawmakers, particularly in the state capitals; there are states in which a city dweller's vote is worth only a twentieth of the vote of an upstate farmhand. Recognizing this situation, Judge John Minor Wisdom, of the New Orleans Court of Appeals, had told the Tuskegee plaintiffs, in effect, that lots of people suffer from being gerrymandered, and that the plaintiffs in Gomillion **v.** Lightfoot couldn't expect the federal courts to step in and help them solely because they were Negroes. "I can see no difference," Judge Wisdom had written bluntly in his opinion, "between partially disfranchising Negroes and partially disfranchising Republicans, Democrats, Italians, Poles, Mexican-Americans, Catholics, bluestocking voters, industrial workers, urban citizens, or other groups who are euchered out of their full suffrage...by gerrymander or malapportionment."

This, then, was how the matter stood as the Supreme Court prepared to take up the case. An authority on constitutional law with whom I had talked had said of it, "I think it's as significant and as tricky a case as has come up in years, because the court is confronted by two apparently conflicting lines of precedent. One line of Supreme Court decisions says that the court may not or should not intervene in questions affecting local political boundaries, such questions not being considered justiciable—that is, capable of resolution in a court of law. The other line says clearly and vigorously that the court will strike down discriminatory laws that deprive persons of some portion of their constitutional rights because of their race, color, or creed. In terms of practical consequences—and the justices are an eminently realistic body of men, who, I believe, give as much weight to practical consequences as they do to legal theory, and sometimes more—the situation is this: If the Negro's condition is to be basically improved in this country, it is crucial that he obtain the voting rights that have long been denied him and that the federal government is now making serious efforts to help him obtain. The question posed by the Tuskegee case is whether the states are going to be permitted to devise ways of vitiating the Negro's voting power after he obtains it. If the Supreme Court follows its precedents in the various gerrymander cases—most notably Justice Frankfurter's opinion in Colegrove v. Green—there is no doubt that its decision will be a great encouragement to states that are determined to keep their Negroes politically impotent. Yet if it rules in favor of the Negroes, what is the court going to do when other kinds of gerrymander victims come before it seeking relief? There are at least half a dozen such complaints pending throughout the country, with attorneys watching very closely to see what the court decides in this case. Is the court going to go all the way into that political thicket at last?"

The Colegrove case, he went on, had concerned the effort of three Illinois voters to prevent their state from conducting elections in their district on the basis of forty-six-year-old population figures; the petitioners had lost by a four-to-three decision. Justices Black and Douglas, who had been in the minority, had long been restive with this decision, on the ground that it perpetuated patent inequities and injustices in the nation's electoral system, thus corrupting democracy at its very core. "They may regard the Tuskegee case, which has the added factor of the racial element, as a prime opportunity for overturning the Colegrove precedent," he said. "They are the court's most vigorous exponents of the philosophy of judicial activism, you know. They tend to hold, if I may simplify a complicated philosophy, that when anything is clearly wrong or unjust, the court ought to do something about it. Justice Frankfurter, on the other hand, takes a much more limited view of the court's proper power and proper function, contending that there are many kinds of abuses that a justice may personally deplore but that it is simply not meet or practical for the court to attempt to rectify. This belief is at the core of his Colegrove opinion—an opinion he is known to cherish highly—and he may be expected to react vigorously and articulately to any challenge to it. But will he defend it at the cost of permitting racial discrimination? That might present him with quite a dilemma. Anyway, it's an intriguing case."

Of this much judicial background I was aware as the argument got under way. It began mildly. The slim young Negro who rose to start presenting the petitioners' case was an attorney from Montgomery,

Alabama, named Fred D. Gray. It was his first appearance before the Supreme Court, and, not surprisingly, he seemed nervous. An easel holding a large map of the area had been brought in by the bailiffs, and Gray, standing before it, presented the basic facts about the old and new boundaries. The justices seemed quite fascinated by the map; they leaned forward, peering at it and seeking to orient themselves, and asked several elementary questions of the sort one might hear from the members of a class in basic map reading. "Now, which part is which on the map?" Justice Stewart asked. "What's been cut out of the city, and what's left in?" It seemed to me that the map, which remained on view throughout the entire presentation of the case, raised and kept before the justices an essential question, one that was to be explored at some length; namely, what reasonable and constitutional purpose could the State of Alabama put forward for devising such a tortuous boundary?

After the map-reading introduction, there were a few more orientation questions from the justices regarding Tuskegee, regarding Tuskegee Institute and its founding in 1881 by Booker T. Washington, and so on—all casual inquiries seeming to stem from ordinary human curiosity rather than from high judicial purpose. Then began the first exploratory probings into the legal issues at stake, beginning with questions about precisely how the plaintiffs could justly claim to have suffered as a result of the boundary revision. Justice Frankfurter wanted to know just what voting rights those who had been put out of the city had lost, and Chief Justice Warren wondered if they had suffered any curtailment of police protection or other essential services. In answer to Justice Frankfurter's question, Gray said that while the petitioners were still entitled to register as voters in Macon County—which meant that they could still help elect county, state, and federal officials—they had been unjustly deprived of the right they had formerly possessed to vote in municipal elections. He then embarked on a recitation of the difficulties that Negroes had encountered in seeking to register to vote in Macon County (difficulties with which I was, of course, familiar after having watched the registration session at the County Courthouse in Tuskegee the day before). But Justice Frankfurter brought Gray up short in the latter's discussion of the county registration situation, interposing, "But that's hardly relevant to the redistricting issue immediately at hand, is it?"

"No, it isn't, sir," said Gray meekly.

On the subject of municipal services, Gray sought earnestly to establish that there had been some perceptible deterioration in the services provided to the Negro sections since the redistricting, but his argument sounded shaky to me, from both the factual and the legal standpoints. (It doesn't take a courtroom spectator long to become a Philadelphia lawyer.) At any rate, the Negroes I had talked with when I was in Tuskegee had not made any point of this as a grievance; they cared deeply about the loss of any portion of their full citizenship rights, but they worried very little over the speed with which their garbage was being collected. Justices Whittaker and Brennan pressed Gray a bit as he floundered along this trail, but on the whole, I thought, the court seemed to treat him quite gently. Even so, Gray appeared greatly relieved when, after he had been on the floor for perhaps fifteen minutes, he was able to announce that he had come to the end of his part of the presentation and that the main burden of the petitioners' argument would be carried forward by a colleague, Robert L. Carter.

With the appearance of Carter, a well-built Negro in his forties who is the general counsel for the National Association for the Advancement of Colored People, the petitioners' case went immediately to the heart of the matter. "Your Honors," Carter said, "our position is simple. This is purely a case of racial discrimination. The purpose of this legislation—Alabama Act 140—was discriminatory. In a manner both callous and deliberate, the state has denied the petitioners their rights solely because they are Negroes." He spoke with simple directness, in a firm, even voice. He looked poised but not relaxed. "Obviously," he went on, "Alabama could not openly disfranchise

Negroes without violating the Constitution. If it had passed a law that had openly denied Negroes, as such, the right to vote in Tuskegee—or the right to live in Tuskegee—there is little question but that this court would strike that law down as unconstitutional. We contend that the same principle applies when the state does these things covertly, as it did in Act 140— a piece of legislation that is as gross a case of racial discrimination as any that has come before this court since Yick Wo versus Hopkins." He was referring to an interesting and important discrimination case that had come before the Supreme Court in 1886. It had its origins in San Francisco, where, in the second half of the nineteenth century, anti-Chinese feeling dominated local politics fully as strongly as the Negro question does in the South today. San Francisco had passed an ordinance stringently regulating public laundries in wooden buildings. The law had made no mention of the Chinese, but, as all San Franciscans well knew, the city's laundry owners were, with few exceptions, Chinese, and their laundries were in wooden buildings, since there were comparatively few buildings in the city of any other material. The Supreme Court held the ordinance to be unconstitutional, saying that despite its appearance of impartiality, it permitted, even invited, a racially biassed result "if it is applied and administered by public authority with an evil eye and an unequal hand."

For Carter, in his present argument, the Yick Wo ruling furnished a powerful and comforting precedent. "We are not contending that Alabama may not change its local boundaries in whatever way it chooses to do so," he went on. "All we say is that it has no right to do so for a discriminatory purpose."

"What's the proof of discrimination here?" drawled a soft Southern voice from behind the stack of books to Chief Justice Warren's right—the voice of Justice Black, a former senator from Alabama, who was born and brought up in rural Clay County, about seventy miles north of Tuskegee. Back in 1937, when Black was first appointed to the Supreme Court, there had been a great uproar over a revelation that he had once belonged, albeit in token fashion, to the Ku Klux Klan; in the years since, however, he had shown himself to be the justice most concerned with protecting the rights and liberties of the individual. Justice Frankfurter, on the other hand, who was regarded by many at the time of his appointment as an extreme liberal, has proved since then to be, in judicial terms, the leading spokesman of the conservative point of view on the court.

"The proof, sir," Carter replied to Justice Black's question, "is the facts as to what the law achieved— the removal of practically every Negro voter from within the city limits, while leaving all the white voters untouched."

" 'Purpose' is, then, the central aspect of your case?" asked Justice Douglas.

"Purpose and effect—the effect reveals the purpose," Carter replied. He started to expand on this, but suddenly the justices were out of their seats and filing from the courtroom. It was four-thirty, quitting time, and the members of the Supreme Court apparently believe in shutting up shop right on the dot.

A few minutes later, in the hall, I saw Carter, and I went over to him and asked how he thought his case was going so far. "Pretty well," he replied carefully. "Not a word from Frankfurter about Colegrove versus Green." His demeanor made me think of a man who has just left the dentist's chair and realizes he hasn't suffered anywhere near the pain he had been dreading, but who isn't going to risk smiling until the Novocain wears off.

A tall, broad-shouldered, hawk-nosed man standing with Carter, whom I surmised to be a fellow attorney, put in, "You'd think Frankfurter had never even *heard* of Colegrove. Did you ever see him so amiable?"

"Well, let's not get overoptimistic," Carter responded. "Tomorrow he may take Colegrove and cut us to ribbons with it."

THE SUPREME COURT CONVENED for its public sessions at noon the next day. I was there in good time, only to find that the arguments on the Tuskegee case were not scheduled to get under way immediately. First, the court held what I learned was a daily ritual —an admission ceremony for lawyers who sought recognition as being qualified to appear before it. After each of these men was introduced by a sponsoring attorney, he was personally welcomed by Chief Justice Warren, in precisely the same friendly tone of voice; then, all together, they took an oath administered by the court clerk. There were eleven initiations on this particular day, and the process seemed to me a needless consumption of time for a body that had so little of it to spare.

As soon as the lawyers and their sponsors had retired, the Chief Justice said, in the same conversational
tone as the day before, "Gomillion versus Lightfoot,"
and Carter stepped forward to carry on. Within five
minutes, the dangerous Colegrove issue, theretofore
quietly caged up, had been let out into the arena for
Carter to try to handle. Unexpectedly, though, it was
not Justice Frankfurter but Justice Black who let it
out. Justice Black set the stage with a couple of soft-
spoken, easygoing queries, apparently devised to provide Carter with the opportunity to restate and clarify
his central position. As the Justice put these questions,
he looked genial and helpful, like a good host at a
dinner party skillfully drawing out one of his guests.
(The books that had been stacked in front of him the
day before had been cleared away, so at last I was
able to see his face.) Then his demeanor changed as
he leaned forward and demanded, "Well, what do
you do about Colegrove? Are you asking us to over-
rule Colegrove?" A thin smile appeared on Justice
Douglas's lips. Down the bench, Justice Frankfurter
put his hands over his eyes, as if suddenly weary. As
for Carter, he had, I'm sure, prepared himself for
this question, but he was obviously perplexed by the
quarter from which it came. Cautiously he said no,
he wasn't asking that the Colegrove ruling be overturned—wasn't asking the court for the kind of blanket
ruling that would render all kinds of gerrymander-

ing and malapportionment unconstitutional—because he didn't think it necessary for his case, which rested on the issue of racial discrimination. However, he added, if it should turn out that the court found the Colegrove precedent an impediment to a favorable decision, then he felt that the Colegrove ruling should indeed be overturned. He was treading most warily here, clearly not wanting to risk having his case obscured by a struggle over a judicial principle.

In his endeavor to tiptoe past Colegrove, Carter was suavely assisted by Justice Frankfurter, who, it had begun to appear, was also concerned with keeping the two issues separate. One had a sense that complicated strategies were involved—for the justices as well as for the attorneys. A series of mild questions from Frankfurter enabled Carter to elucidate the various ways in which the Tuskegee gerrymander could be regarded as a clear case of racial discrimination. When Carter had concluded, Justice Frankfurter said "Ah, yes," went on to sum up all of Carter's points cogently, and then swivelled about in his chair and surveyed his colleagues. This last action was one I had noticed before. On occasions when he had raised a subtle or significant point, he would glance around at the other justices, as if to assure himself that they had perceived all its jurisprudential nuances. I was reminded of a comment about Justice Frankfurter that had once been made to me by a lawyer who had argued numerous cases before the Supreme Court. "The fact that he's a Supreme Court justice hasn't caused Frankfurter to cease being a Harvard law professor," he said. "All the time he's up there on the bench, he's educating people in the law—counsel, his fellow justices, everyone. He's dressed me down on some occasions as if I were a first-year student without a chance of passing." The lawyer had laughed, then added, "The court is going to be a much duller place when the time comes for Frankfurter to retire."

Several justices now addressed themselves in various ways to defining the nature of a "constitutional deprivation." Referring to the population statistics around which the petitioners had built much of their case, Justice Black asked, "What difference does it make whether four hundred Negro voters are excluded, or four thousand, or four—or just one?" Carter replied that indeed, it made no difference in principle, and that in his view the law would be just as unconstitutional if it had deliberately excluded only one Negro voter, but that since nowhere in the Tuskegee redistricting act was race mentioned in explicit terms, the lopsided before-and-after statistics reflecting the exclusion of Negroes from Tuskegee made it easier for him to prove his contention that the law was racist in inspiration and purpose. The statistics, he said, were in the brief to supply evidence, not to set forth a principle. He implied that he might

have had a much harder time proving that the essential
purpose of Alabama Act 140 was discriminatory if
the Alabama legislators had been subtler, or more
cagey, as they went about framing the law. I reflected
now that if the legislators had redrawn the city's
boundaries in such a way as to exclude a smaller
number of the Negro voters, and had excluded at least
a token number of whites, they could still have
achieved the purpose frankly stated to me by just
about every white Tuskegeean with whom I had
spoken—namely, to keep political power firmly in
white hands—but they would perhaps have run less risk
of being checked by the courts. This train of thought
led me to speculate, as I had often done in Tuskegee
the week before, on what could have led the whites in
power to be so blatant about what they were doing.
Did they really believe that their subterfuge would
stand up in the courts, because of Colegrove and other
legal precedents? If so, was it a matter of pride to
make the subterfuge just as transparent as possible,
so as to show *them* a thing or two—*them* being the
Negroes, the federal courts, the Commission on Civil
Rights, the North, world opinion, the whole vague
complex of forces that has ganged up, in the opinion
of much of the white South, to destroy its cherished
way of life? Or, to conjecture still further, and more
tenuously, was it possible that in making their bill
more extreme than it needed to be, the Alabama

legislators, like a child throwing a temper tantrum, secure in the knowledge that responsible adults will save him from the consequences of his extreme behavior, were unconsciously seeking to make it inevitable that their actions would be checked and reproved? To an outside observer, most of the Southern legislation on the racial question—such as the forty-six bills on school segregation passed by recent sessions of the Louisiana State Legislature, all of which were ultimately declared unconstitutional by the federal courts, as everyone had known they would be—would seem to fall into this temper-tantrum category.

In cases that raise large constitutional questions and are deemed to have a serious effect on the national interest, the United States Solicitor General or one of his deputies may appear on behalf of one side or the other in the capacity of *amicus curiae,* or friend of the court. Gomillion v. Lightfoot was considered to be such a case, and when Carter had concluded his argument, his place before the justices was taken by Assistant Solicitor General Philip Elman, who was there to express the concern of the United States government on behalf of the Negro plaintiffs. A heavy-set, brown-haired, bespectacled man, Elman was dressed in cutaway and striped trousers, his uniform on these occasions. He took up, with practiced competence, the various legal questions that the justices addressed to him, but it shortly became evident that he was moved to express not only a legal stand but also a moral one—not only to adduce that Alabama Act 140 was unconstitutional but to convey as strongly as possible the fact that he considered it downright wrong, and that it outraged him as a human being. "This is the most fundamental thing you can have," he reminded the justices at one point. "People are coming to you and saying, 'We are being deprived of our most cherished rights simply because we're colored.' " For the justices to ignore this appeal on some formalistic ground, he said, would be for them to show, in the phrase that Justice Frankfurter had used in an earlier discrimination case, "the blindness of indifference rather than the blindness of impartiality." Perhaps his most eloquent passage came during a colloquy with Justice Whittaker, in response to the Justice's observation that the Negroes affected by the act hadn't actually lost their voting rights, because they could still vote outside of the city, and there was nothing in the Constitution guaranteeing every American citizen a right to vote in a municipality. Even if they had lost nothing whatever, Elman responded, the creation of a situation of Apartheid was intolerable. It was in the mere conception of a racial boundary line that the essence of the act's unconstitutionality lay. "I find it inconceivable," he said, "that in the year 1960 any defense of a law establishing a ghetto in the United States could be seriously asserted in this court." On the question of whether the Negroes who were now outside the Tuskegee city limits enjoyed the same public services as before, he had one comment to make: "If people live in a ghetto, it makes no difference that their houses might be finer than those outside."

It was interesting to compare the demeanor of Elman, the legal representative of the United States government, the man in the cutaway, with that of the two Negro attorneys, who, though they certainly cared no less deeply than he about the injustice of racial discrimination, had taken some trouble not to show their feelings. Carter, to be sure, had been vigorous and forthright in explaining his legal position, but that was not quite the same thing. It was as if the fact of their being Negroes themselves put them, in this case, under a kind of constraint that a white lawyer was not subjected to—as if they felt it incumbent on them to be more on their dignity, or perhaps to keep a tighter rein on their emotions. They seemed to wish to stress the professional objectivity of their advocacy and to minimize any suggestion of personal pleading.

In the course of his argument, Elman, too, encountered some sticky spots. They were the work of

Justice Douglas, who hitherto had said little. "Would you make the same argument if this were a school-boundary case?" Douglas asked, in a dry but rather challenging voice, as Elman was expanding on his premise that the Constitution forbids the federal and state governments to draw any color line whatever in their legislation. "What if the line had long existed? Say this were the classic pattern of the school cases and those who were out were trying to get in?" Elman managed to field this and similar questions from Douglas well enough—essentially by making the point that if there were all blacks on one side of a line and all whites on the other, the presumption must be that at some time in the past there had been "at least a prima-facie unconstitutionality" and that the burden should be on the state to demonstrate that such a line had actually been drawn in non-discriminatory fashion originally. Such is basically the assumption in cases, he said, "where it may appear that over a period of years, in a particular area, no Negro has ever served on a jury. This may, at least theoretically, be the result of fortuitous factors. But, nonetheless, in those cases the state has been compelled to meet the heavy burden, if it can, of overcoming the normal, commonsense presumption that the reason Negroes do not appear on juries is that they are being systematically excluded."

Justice Douglas nodded—a rather cryptic nod,

not necessarily a gesture of assent—and Elman went on to another aspect of the case. He had apparently coped successfully enough with the questions Justice Douglas had tossed at him, but he looked somewhat perturbed. Just as Carter had been when Justice Black had challenged him, Elman seemed rather puzzled at the unexpected direction from which his trickiest challenges had come.

Elman's remarks concluded the petitioners' side of the argument, and it was now the turn of the respondents—the representatives of the Tuskegee and Alabama authorities. Their argument was made by an Alabama lawyer with an easygoing, folksy manner— a ruddy-faced man of about fifty, bald except for a fringe of gray hair at the back of his head. His name was James J. Carter. There had been occasions earlier in the proceedings—particularly during one discussion in which a number of references were made hypothetically to "Black Tuskegee" and "White Tuskegee"—when the case had seemed to take on something of the aspect of a modern morality play, and this suggestion was reinforced now, as I learned that the two sides were represented by counsel with the same surname. A Black Carter and a White Carter opposing each other was the kind of device that a dramatic moralist might have used in order to remind audiences of the common humanity of two antagonists.

White Carter couldn't see what all the fuss was about. This case, his relaxed, amiable air conveyed, was a mighty big to-do over a little-bitty thing like a municipal-boundary revision. The new Tuskegee, he submitted, was "not too unusual a looking outfit" compared to other cities, in spite of all the emphasis that had been placed on the peculiar outline of its many-sided boundary. He said that just the previous evening he had been thumbing through a Rand McNally atlas in his hotel room and had found lots of cities with shapes that were just as interesting. "Cincinnati looks like a jigsaw puzzle," he told the justices, "and Scranton, Pennsylvania, looks sort of like a cloud." Then he reminded the court that "an unbroken line of decisions by this Honorable Court and other courts" supported his position that a state legislature has absolute discretion in regard to the boundaries of municipalities, without hindrance or interference by the federal courts. "I don't say I've got a white-horse case," he said, invoking a picturesque image I had never heard before, "but I do think I've got the law." He had ample precedents to cite: Hunter v. Pittsburgh (in which the Supreme Court had declared emphatically, "We have nothing to do with the policy, wisdom, justice, or fairness of the act under consideration; those questions are for the consideration of those to whom the state has entrusted its legislative power, and their determination of them is not subject to review or criticism by this Court"), Laramie County v. Albany County, Mount Pleasant v. Beckwith, and Kelly v. Pittsburgh (for some reason, Pittsburgh seems to have been a breeding ground for boundary-dispute cases). In summarizing these cases, the Alabamian managed to make them quite lively and real: ". . . and then there was the case of Mr. Kelly. He was a farmer, and he was taken into the city of Pittsburgh when its boundaries were revised. Mr. Kelly complained that he had to pay twenty-one hundred dollars in taxes, and he said, 'I haven't got no more than four hundred dollars income from the property.' Mr. Kelly was most unhappy at being taken into the city without his consent. He went all the way to the Supreme Court on this, but the court wouldn't give him satisfaction."

"You are saying that the creation, destruction, or modification of a municipality is the prerogative and jurisdiction of the state alone," Justice Frankfurter observed. "Is that correct?"

"That's a fair statement of my position," Carter replied. His case, he went on, rested on three grounds: first, on the state's lawful power to regulate boundaries, which he had just taken up; second, on the ground that the motive of a law could not be inquired into; and, third, on the ground that the federal courts had enunciated the principle of judicial self-restraint in regard to issues such as the present one.

Justice Whittaker asked, "Could this lawful power you speak of be used to accomplish an unlawful purpose?"

Carter's reply was that the state legislatures and state court systems are, and must remain, the only legitimate sources of redress for any injustice that might happen to be inflicted in such instances, and that this principle had been maintained even in a case such as Benson v. United States, "where a man had been on trial for his very life, but where the federal courts declared they lacked the jurisdiction to intervene."

Continuing, the Alabama counsel said, "To come to intent, there is nothing to construe in this case. These are the boundary lines—period. That's all that Act 140 states. When you come to inquiring into motive—and 'motive' is what's meant here rather than 'intent'—it just can't be done. You go back to the very beginnings of this country—to Fletcher v. Peck—where a Georgia state law was being challenged and it was alleged that a Georgia legislator had been bribed to vote for it, and Chief Justice Marshall said, no, you can't inquire into why the legislators voted for that law but can only examine the law itself."

"Suppose that the statute we are here considering had explicitly stated that its purpose was to preserve segregation," Justice Harlan said. "Would you still be maintaining the same position here?"

"No, sir," the Alabama lawyer replied frankly, and then added, in a conversational manner, "Our state's constitution was based on segregation, you know. We well understand there's been a change of climate since then. But, in fact, nothing of that sort is to be found in the law. Some territory has been simply detached from a municipal corporation—and that is all that the law states or that can be read into it."

Justice Frankfurter leaned forward and commented crisply, "Your answer to Justice Harlan makes inroads on your proposition."

The Alabama attorney didn't attempt a direct refutation of this comment. "I don't speak for the state," he said easily, like a good raconteur picking up the thread of his story after an unfortunate interruption, "but if any legislature should be foolish enough to put that in a law nowadays it *should* be knocked down." His remark brought a laugh in the courtroom, and smiles to the lips of some of the justices. It was the first, and the only, faintly humorous moment of the case. The jest seemed to be aimed at taking everyone in the courtroom, including the justices, into a kind of clubby fellowship of those who knew that among men of the world it was assumed to be all right to do certain things as long as you used some subterfuge to avoid getting into trouble.

Chief Justice Warren spoke up. "You said motive can't be inquired into. Would you say that results can be inquired into?"

"There's an awfully shady distinction there," the Alabama lawyer replied carefully. He said that he thought it would be an encroachment for the courts to make such inquires in a case like this, "where the boundaries have been drawn in a manner compatible with the laws of Alabama."

"Suppose the results are *in*compatible with the Constitution of the United States?" Chief Justice Warren said. He had asked only a few questions during the case, none of them remarkably subtle or learned, but the quality of solemn, elemental majesty in his presence made it seem, when he did ask a question, in his booming voice, somewhat as if Mount Rushmore had spoken. Now, in the face of this massive, simple query, the Alabama lawyer seemed to wilt perceptibly.

"I don't believe they are," he answered.

"Isn't that all the petitioners are asking—to have an inquiry made so as to find out if they are?" the Chief Justice said.

"They're asking to go into motive," the Alabamian said. Now he reached—with some haste, I thought —for the comfort of the Colegrove precedent. "This is about as highly political a thing as we can get into

—local boundaries," he declared, and he reminded the justices of the principle of judicial self-limitation that they had asserted in such cases, and of the threat that if they failed to maintain that principle, they would find themselves up to their ears in local politics. Should the federal courts be expected to step in and tell the states exactly where they should draw the boundary lines for each locality, he asked, and what percentages of white and colored people the lines should include?

In an argument before the Supreme Court, the petitioners' side gets the last word, because it has a greater burden than the respondents', in that it is seeking to have lower-court decisions overturned. So when White Carter concluded, Black Carter came forward to refute him. He was brief about it. He said again that the matter at hand was not an abstract question of local boundaries but a clear-cut instance of racial discrimination. And as for the suggestion that if his side won, the federal courts would have the impossible task of drawing local boundary lines, he countered it by calmly stating that all that was being asked in this case was that the Tuskegee line, drawn to achieve a racially discriminatory end, be declared unconstitutional, and that the city's boundaries revert to what they were before. There, without any flourish or dramatic climax, he ended his presentation. Again there occurred the quick stir of movement I had observed the day before. A new group of lawyers came forward and took the places of those who had been at the front tables; the Chief Justice called "United States versus Mississippi Valley Generating Company"; and the Supreme Court of the United States promptly turned its attention from the question of voting rights in Tuskegee, Alabama, to the question of conflict of interest in the negotiation of a contract for the Atomic Energy Commission.

Upon leaving the courtroom, I encountered White Carter, the Alabama lawyer, in the hall, and asked him how he thought things had gone.

"Very well," he said cheerfully. "I've never seen the justices give a case more searching scrutiny. I won't try to predict what the outcome will be, but certainly it's been a fascinating case."

I asked if there had been any surprises.

He laughed, and said, "Not for me. I think opposing counsel ran into some, though."

Shortly thereafter, I met Assistant Solicitor General Elman in the ground-floor cafeteria of the courthouse, and we discussed the case over a snack. First of all, he confirmed White Carter's assertion that there had been surprises for the petitioners' lawyers. "It's astonishing, the way it went," he said. "Frankfurter, whom we thought about with trepidation as we prepared the case, couldn't have been gentler. Our sharpest attack came from the court's great activists—from the two justices whom the public would naturally expect to be most sympathetic to the petitioners' claims in a civil-rights case like this. Furthermore, they attacked us along lines that didn't seem to me to go to the central problem before the court and that I don't think they need have gone into at all."

This led Elman into some inconclusive speculation about whether Justices Black and Douglas, by their sharp questioning, had been attempting to broaden the issue beyond the racial question, so as to use the case as a wedge for breaching the entire judicial blockade against discussion of gerrymanders. At the end of it, he shook his head. "I don't know what they were driving at," he said. Then he went on to talk about the court in general, and as he did so, his perturbation left him and he began to glow with enthusiasm. He had once been a law clerk of Justice Frankfurter's, I learned, and since 1946 had appeared before the court in a great number of cases, but his familiarity with the court and with the inevitable human frailties beneath the impersonal black robes of justice appeared to have bred not contempt but increasing admiration. "It seems to me a superb process, this informal, reflective questioning conducted by men who have studied the matter at hand and are seeking to get to the heart of it," he said. "I wish that candidates for President, instead of engaging in TV debates, could be put through this kind of questioning process, by these very justices. Then we'd end up *knowing* something about the candidates and their positions on the issues. Yes, it's a great institution, the court, and"—he laughed—"to my mind, the best show in Washington."

I asked if he cared to venture a prediction on how the court would rule in Gomillion v. Lightfoot. He replied without hesitation, "Certainly. When one tries to guess the outcome of a case, he can't merely analyze the various precedents, or weigh the conflicting arguments, or speculate as to what the justices may be thinking on the basis of the questions they have asked during the argument. You have to consider what the consequences of the alternative rulings might be. The Supreme Court justices are a realistic and sophisticated group of men. When they weigh a constitutional or civil-rights case, they are not engaged —as laymen tend to think—in a mere legalistic scrutiny of precedents. Justices must also take into account the effect their rulings will have on the country's welfare and the values it lives by. And in those terms, in this Tuskegee case, no matter what arguments we've heard or what surprises may have occurred in some of the justices' questions, it's absolutely inconceivable to me that in this present era the court could rule in favor of the respondents and sanction so blatant a racial discrimination. I just can't conceive of it."

W HEN THE COURT'S RULING was handed down, twenty-seven days later—a surprisingly speedy decision in a major case of such complexity and delicacy—it justified the vehement certainty of Elman's prediction. The decision was in favor of the petitioners and it was unanimous. The opinion was written by Justice Frankfurter. Its language was incisive. It said that the Tuskegee Negroes were entitled to a full court trial on the merits of their case, that their allegations, if proved at such a trial, "would abundantly establish that Act 140 was not an ordinary geographic redistricting measure even within familiar abuses of gerrymandering," and that "if these allegations upon a trial remained uncontradicted or unqualified, the conclusion would be irresistible, tantamount for all practical purposes to a mathematical demonstration, that the legislation is solely concerned with segregating white and colored voters by fencing Negro citizens out of town so as to deprive them of their preexisting municipal vote." The opinion continued, "It is difficult to appreciate what stands in the way of adjudging a statute having this inevitable effect invalid in light of the principles by which this Court must judge, and uniformly has judged, statutes that, howsoever speciously defined, obviously discriminate against colored citizens." Here Justice Frankfurter quoted, without a credit, from one of his favorite authors—himself: "The [Fifteenth] Amendment nullifies sophisticated as well as simple-minded modes of discrimination"—an eminently quotable dictum that he had originally asserted in a court opinion in 1939.

"The complaint amply alleges a claim of racial discrimination," Justice Frankfurter's decision continued. "Against this claim the respondents have never suggested, either in their brief or in oral argument, any countervailing municipal function which Act 140 is designed to serve. The respondents invoke generalities expressing the state's unrestricted power —unlimited, that is, by the United States Constitution —to establish, destroy, or reorganize by contraction or expansion its political subdivisions, to wit, cities, counties, and other local units. We freely recognize the breadth and importance of this aspect of the state's political power. To exalt this power into an absolute is to misconceive the reach and rule of this Court's decisions in the leading case of Hunter v. Pittsburgh, 207 U.S. 161, and related cases relied upon by respondents."

Those cases, the opinion declared, had essentially involved property disputes, and had hinged on the question of contractual obligations. None of them had involved racial discrimination or any violation of a federally protected right. In short, Justice Frankfurter said, "When a state exercises power wholly within the domain of state interest, it is insulated from federal judicial review. But such insulation is not carried over when state power is used as an instrument for circumventing a federally protected right."

The pithiest language of the opinion was that in which Justice Frankfurter rejected the respondents' attempt to invoke him as an ally by citing his Colegrove opinion. He spurned the parallel between the Colegrove case and the present one, saying that the great difference was the specific singling out of "a readily isolated segment of a racial minority for special discriminatory treatment." "And," he went on, "according to the allegations here made, the Alabama Legislature has not merely redrawn the Tuskegee city limits with incidental inconvenience to the petitioners; it is more accurate to say that it has deprived the petitioners of the municipal franchise and consequent rights, and to that end it has incidentally changed the city's boundaries. While in form this is merely an act redefining metes and bounds, if the allegations are established, the inescapable human effect of this essay in geometry and geography is to despoil colored citizens, and only colored citizens, of their theretofore enjoyed voting rights. That was not Colegrove v. Green."

Along with Justice Frankfurter's opinion, there was a brief concurring one by Justice Whittaker, who said that he agreed with the court's judgment but that it seemed to him the decision should be rested not on the Fifteenth Amendment, which concerns the right to vote, but on the equal-protection clause of the Fourteenth Amendment, which was the basis of the school-segregation decisions. He took care to add that his thesis, "incidentally, clearly would not involve, just as the cited [school-segregation] cases did not involve, the Colegrove problem."

That this indeed remains a problem for the court could be discerned in a cryptic postscript to Justice Frankfurter's opinion, which read, "Mr. Justice Douglas, while joining the opinion of the Court, adheres to the dissents in Colegrove v. Green, 328 U.S. 549, and South v. Peters, 339 U.S. 276."

The court would have further opportunity to confront the gerrymander problem, for since the Tuskegee decision a Tennessee case that contains no element of racial discrimination but concerns legislative malapportionment only has come up before it, and this was slated to be heard the next term.

While the Tuskegee gerrymander case was in process, another legal attempt to give Negroes in the area access to the ballot box was being carried on by the federal Justice Department. This effort was directed against the Macon County Board of Registrars, who were accused of strictly limiting, by means of delaying tactics and various other devices, the number of Negroes permitted to register to vote (including many with Ph.D. degrees), while at the same time registering without hindrance whites who were illiterate. This was the board I had watched in action—if "action" is the right word—on one of the days I was in Tuskegee. I had been told then that only about a thousand of an estimated fourteen thousand Negroes of voting age in Macon County were registered; and since then the United States Commission on Civil Rights has ascertained that in 1960, although Macon County had only 2,818 eligible whites, there were 3,310 names of whites on the voting rolls—one hundred and seventeen per cent representation. In March, 1961 the government's suit against the Macon County Board of Registrars finally came to trial in Montgomery before

United States District Judge Frank M. Johnson, Jr., who issued a sweeping ruling ordering the board to cease discriminating and to speed up its procedures. Specifically, Judge Johnson directed, among other things, that a number of obviously qualified Negroes be registered at once; that fifty words be the maximum any applicant need be required to read and write in order to prove his literacy; that applicants must be informed within twenty days after their examination whether they have passed or failed, and if they have failed, for what reason (hitherto it had been the board's practice not to bother to notify Negroes whom it was rejecting); and, finally, that the board was to report its progress to the court once a month. Henceforth, in Judge Johnson's words, the board could not refuse to register any Negro "whose performance in attempting to qualify is equal to the performance of the least qualified white applicant ever registered."

A few weeks earlier, this same Judge Johnson, abiding by the principles the Supreme Court had enunciated in Justice Frankfurter's opinion, had ruled Alabama Act 140 unconstitutional and ordered that Tuskegee's boundaries revert to what they had been before. The matter was considered so open-and-shut, in fact, that the Judge issued this ruling merely on the basis of the written briefs submitted by opposing counsel, without listening to any oral argument.

Thus ended three and a half years of litigation in the case of Gomillion v. Lightfoot.

Some months later, after I had allowed time for both of Judge Johnson's decrees to take effect, I called up Professor Gomillion at Tuskegee Institute to find out how he felt about the legal victories, and to ask him about the general atmosphere prevailing between whites and Negroes in the aftermath of the court rulings. He was cautiously optimistic. "The mayor we have now, Howard Rutherford, seems to want to be open-minded," he said, in the level, careful tones that I recalled from our previous conversations. "He's said he'll oppose any attempt to reopen the gerrymander question, and that he intends to treat all of the town's citizens, white and black, fairly. The board has been registering about twenty Negroes at each session, and although we still think we're encountering some needless hindrances, it's certainly an extraordinary change. So all the litigation has been worthwhile."

I asked him if there had been any threat of violence, for shortly before I spoke with him there had occurred the riots in Birmingham and Montgomery against the Freedom Riders.

"No," he said, "not in Tuskegee. And we don't anticipate any, though I may be being over-optimistic.

117

Conceivably, trouble of some sort might develop as Negro voters in the city approach parity with the whites. That's the prospect, of course, that gives the white politicians nightmares, no matter how we insist that we don't intend to run a Negro slate of candidates, and that all we want is a situation in which there can be representation on the basis of merit, not of color. So it's possible that, out of panic, they might take some drastic action—not physical violence, necessarily, but something like abolishing Macon County altogether and dispersing it among its neighboring counties—an action, as you know, that's already been authorized by a state referendum, and that's being held as a reserve weapon to be used if the legislature decides the Negroes here are pressing too hard for their rights. We hope that, because of the Gomillion versus Lightfoot decision, the politicians will see the folly and uselessness of such a move and not try it. But you can't be sure what panicky people will do. It's possible that in the immediate future things are going to get worse, here and throughout the state. But it's my feeling that within a few years after that they're going to get much better." He paused, then added, very carefully, "I hope I'm not wrong about that."

(continued from front flap)

known as Gomillion *et al. versus* Lightfoot *et al.*—Gomillion being a professor at Tuskegee Institute, and Lightfoot the city's mayor. Slowly the case began to work its way up through the court system.

In the fall of 1960, Bernard Taper, one of the leading reporters for *The New Yorker* magazine, traveled first to Tuskegee and later to Washington in order to skillfully weave together the background material and the entire case. When he was finished, Mr. Taper had written a moving and significant book.

He met Charles G. Gomillion and the faculty of Tuskegee Institute, and he records their feelings with the same candor he devotes to Mayor Philip M. Lightfoot, and other white townspeople who found themselves involved in a conflict of far greater import and consequence than they had conceived. Finally, Mr. Taper stood an entire day with Tuskegee Negroes, many of them with Ph.D. degrees, as they vainly attempted to register, and he vividly contrasts their patient insistence with the manifest uneasiness of the registrars.

When Gomillion *v.* Lightfoot came up before the Supreme Court, Mr. Taper left for Washington. Step by step, as the case unfolds, he re-creates the growing tension and drama while the lawyers argue their causes and answer the frank, often surprising questions asked by the Justices. With a rare talent and insight, Mr. Taper explores the character of the Justices, especially that of Felix Frankfurter, and underscores what a favorable or unfavorable decision will mean to Court precedent.

Gomillion versus Lightfoot is much more than a thoughtful and unbiased report on one of the most important cases to come before the Supreme Court. It is an examination of a racial crisis in a small Southern town, brought to life by a gifted and most distinguished journalist.

Printed in the USA
CPSIA information can be obtained
at www.ICGtesting.com
LVHW021455070124
768338LV00003B/330